More Praise for *Organic Church*

"In an age where millions are saying 'God yes, church no!' most of us instinctively feel that church as we know it prevents church as God wants it. But where, exactly, is the catch? Where do we go from here? Neil Cole expertly places a thrilling invitation before us to join probably the most exciting spiritual pilgrimage going on today: the global migration of a church on the way back home. Come and dial in!"
—Wolfgang Simson, author, *Houses That Change the World*

"Church multiplication is not likely to be the province of ivory tower theoreticians! In *Organic Church* Neil Cole helps us to understand that church multiplication is never going to be a spectator sport. This is hands down the most useful and comprehensive book currently available to understanding the rapidly growing expressions of simple, organic church life around the world."
—Dr. N. A. (Tony) Dale, editor, *House 2 House Magazine*

"I heartily recommend this book. It is packed with deep insights; you will find no fluff in it. Among the books on church planting, it offers a rare combination of attributes: it is biblical and well written, its model has proven effective, and it is authored by a practitioner rather than an observer or an ivory-tower theoretician."
—Curtis Sergeant, directory of church planting,
Saddleback Church, Lake Forest, California

"It is a great joy to recommend Neil Cole's *Organic Church*. The stories and experiences in this book will encourage many to follow the Holy Spirit and go where God is leading. Neil Cole is a true pioneer in the faith and a man of great vision who has chosen to live out the things that God has poured into him. I believe this book will ignite hearts to live out their faith in organic communities across the country and around the world."
—Rev. Michael Steele, North American director,
Dawn Ministries

"Neil Cole is a true trailblazer for today's church. His story will inspire you and equip you to experience the living Christ in community."

—Jonathan S. Campbell, Ph.D., author, *The Way of Jesus*

Organic Church

Organic Church

Growing Faith Where Life Happens

Neil Cole

Foreword by Leonard Sweet

JOSSEY-BASS

Organic Church

Growing Faith Where Life Happens

Neil Cole

Foreword by Leonard I. Sweet

A Leadership Network publication

JOSSEY-BASS
A Wiley Imprint
www.josseybass.com

Published by Jossey-Bass
A Wiley Imprint
989 Market Street, San Francisco, CA 94103-1741   www.josseybass.com

Jossey-Bass books and products are available through most bookstores. To contact Jossey-Bass directly call our Customer Care Department within the U.S. at 800-956-7739, outside the U.S. at 317-572-3986, or fax 317-572-4002.

Jossey-Bass also publishes its books in a variety of electronic formats. Some content that appears in print may not be available in electronic books.

Scripture taken from the HOLY BIBLE, NEW INTERNATIONAL VERSION®. NIV®. Copyright © 1973, 1978, 1984 by International Bible Society. Used by permission of Zondervan. All rights reserved.

Scripture quotations taken from the New American Standard Bible®, Copyright © 1960, 1962, 1963, 1968, 1971, 1972, 1973, 1975, 1977, 1995 by The Lockman Foundation. Used by permission." (www.Lockman.org)

Photo on page 97, two-day-old human embryo at four-cell stage of development x260, Stone/Yorgos Nikas

Photos on page 128, Forest Ferns, PhotoDisc, Inc.

Photo on page 128, Fern, PhotoDisc/Getty Images

Library of Congress Cataloging-in-Publication Data

Cole, Neil, date.
Organic church: growing faith where life happens / Neil Cole; foreword by Leonard Sweet.—
1st ed.
p. cm.
Includes bibliographical references and index.
ISBN-13: 978-0-7879-8129-7 (alk. paper)
ISBN-10: 0-7879-8129-X (alk. paper)
1. Church renewal. 2. Evangelistic work. 3. Christianity and culture. I. Title.
BV600.3.C64 2005
250—dc22
2005015652

Printed in the United States of America
FIRST EDITION
HB Printing   10 9 8 7 6 5 4 3 2 1

Leadership Network Titles

112092

Contents

About Leadership Network

Since 1984, Leadership Network has fostered church innovation and growth by diligently pursuing its far-reaching mission statement: to identify, connect, and help high-capacity Christian leaders multiply their impact.

Although Leadership Network's techniques adapt and change as the church faces new opportunities and challenges, the organization's work follows a consistent and proven pattern.

Leadership Network brings together entrepreneurial leaders who are focused on similar ministry initiatives. The ensuing collaboration—often across denominational lines—creates a strong base from which individual leaders can better analyze and refine their own strategies. Peer-to-peer interaction, dialogue, and sharing inevitably accelerate participants' innovation and ideas. Leadership Network further enhances this process through developing and distributing highly targeted ministry tools and resources, including audio and video programs, special reports, e-publications, and online downloads.

With Leadership Network's assistance, today's Christian leaders are energized, equipped, inspired, and better able to multiply their own dynamic Kingdom-building initiatives.

Launched in 1996 in conjunction with Jossey-Bass (a Wiley imprint), Leadership Network Publications present thoroughly researched and innovative concepts from leading thinkers, practitioners, and pioneering churches. The series collectively draws from a range of disciplines, with individual titles offering perspective on one or more of five primary areas:

1. Enabling effective leadership
2. Encouraging life-changing service
3. Building authentic community
4. Creating Kingdom-centered impact
5. Engaging cultural and demographic realities

For additional information on the mission or activities of Leadership Network, please contact:

Leadership Network
2501 Cedar Springs, Suite 200
Dallas, TX 75201
(800) 765–5323
client.care@leadnet.org

Foreword

Davidson's Mains, also known as Muttonhole, is a Scottish village about three miles northwest of Edinburgh. While there to lead a one-day advance with young leaders from the Church of Scotland, I was befriended by my host, Jerry Middleton, the pastor of the parish kirk. One of the gifts he gave me was his recounting of an experience he had had a few months earlier.

While walking his parish one day in his clerical garb, a couple of kids called to him from across the street, "Hey, mister, would you stop being a minister long enough to give us a hand?" Stunned by the words but braced for the challenge, Jerry crossed the street. When he arrived on their side he found that the chain of one of their bikes had broken and needed to be fixed. So he knelt down right there on the sidewalk and started to dismantle the bike and remove the chain. The two young brothers couldn't believe that this minister would actually get down to help them. And they were even more surprised when he proved skilled at fixing their problem.

When he had finished repairing the bicycle, they apologized for making him get his hands so filthy with oil and grease. Jerry shrugged it off. "No problem, fellas. Want to learn how to get off grime like this?" "No way," one of them said, "you can't get that off here."

"Let me show you," Jerry continued. Once again he got down on the ground, but this time he gathered up dirt and "washed" his hands in some loose soil. After he scrubbed the dirt into his hands, he turned to them and said, "Do you know where we can find some water?" The boys said, "We live right around the corner. Come with us."

So the three of them went marching right into the kitchen of their house, much to the surprise of their mother, who was asked to move over at the sink as she stood openmouthed at the strange priest her children had brought home with them. "Thank you for letting me wash my hands here," Jerry said as the boys watched the water work its magic on his hands, restoring them to spotless purity. The mother then asked him to stay for tea. Jerry confessed that this was "one of the strangest pastoral calls" he had ever made, but he also professed to having learned a lot about ministry in a postmodern culture from this one incident.

It was not until I finished reading Neil Cole's fabulous Introduction to *Organic Church* that I began to understand the profound significance of Jerry's story. This is a post-Christian culture that doesn't think the church has anything to offer it except when we stop doing church the way we've been doing it: "Hey, mister, would you stop being a minister long enough to give us a hand?" People today aren't coming over to the Christian side of the street. We have to cross over to their side if we're to give a hand. And ministry happens best not in planned ways but naturally, organically and often when we're on our way to do something else.

I love how Neil Cole puts it: "If you want to win this world to Christ, you are going to have to sit in the smoking section." If the church isn't willing to get its hands (or lungs) dirty, it won't have a hearing. The homes and hearts of people are open to the Gospel. But it's relationships that bring the Gospel home. The church is at its best in two's or three's—not in two or three hundreds or two or three thousands. "Where two or three are gathered together, there am I in the midst of them."

Organic Church is less about what we are to do than a book about what God has already done and now is doing. I challenge you to put it down without the picture of what God intended the church to be, becoming a hologram in your heart. Read it and reap a harvest of seeds ready to plant. Read it and weep a harvest of tears at what could be if we were to, as Cole puts it so memorably, "lower the bar of how church is done and raise the bar of what it means to be a disciple." The real sin is not what happened in the past. The real sin is what is *not* happening in the present.

> Dr. Leonard I. Sweet
> E. Stanley Jones Chair in Evangelism
> Drew University

This work is dedicated to two generations in my life. First, to the memory of Ray Walker, who showed me what it means to be a man who loves Jesus and others. Second, to Heather, Erin, Zachary, and the next generation of Kingdom agents, who will take the church to new places we never dreamed possible.

Preface

It's raining very hard this night. Neo is escorted by a strange group of countercultural misfits. Part geek, part chic, they act as though they are smarter than the rest of the world.

Neo is controlled at gunpoint and taken to an old abandoned building under the promise of meeting the infamous Morpheus. Here he will be offered some pills from a dark stranger wearing reflective sunglasses and a black trench coat—*and he will willingly swallow one of the pills!*

What would compel him to do so? He is driven by a desire he can no longer resist. An insatiable curiosity and a holy dissatisfaction with the norm push him to abandon restraint. He is motivated to take extraordinary risks now because he can no longer stay in the dull world of normal life . . . of business as usual.

There are polite greetings. Then a most interesting dialogue ensues.

Morpheus begins by describing Neo's plight as similar to Alice falling down the rabbit hole in Lewis Carroll's story. He comments that Neo has the look of one who accepts only what he sees because he is in a dream and about to awaken, which is ironically very close to the truth. Morpheus tells Neo why they brought him here. It is his chance to learn what the Matrix is; Morpheus asks if he wants to know.

Neo nods slowly, but without hesitation, as if realizing that this is a turning point in his life, marking a change forever. Morpheus explains: "The Matrix is everywhere. It is all around us, even now in this very room. You can see it when you look out your window, or when you turn on your television. You can feel it when you go to work, when you go to church, when you pay your taxes. It is the world that has been pulled over your eyes to blind you to the truth."

Neo inquires as to what truth Morpheus is referring to.

"That you are a slave, Neo. Like everyone else, you were born into bondage, born into a prison that you cannot smell or taste or touch. A prison for your mind."

Morpheus opens a small silver box, takes two pills from it, and informs Neo that mere description is not enough; he must see it for himself to understand. Morpheus then leans forward, with a pill in each hand.

"This is your last chance. After this, there is no going back. You take the blue pill, the story ends, you wake up in your bed and believe whatever you want to. You take the red pill, you stay in Wonderland, and I show you how deep the rabbit hole goes."

Neo slowly yet deliberately reaches for the red pill.

Morpheus suddenly tells him that he is offering only the truth, nothing more. Neo takes and swallows the red pill, and the adventure begins.

He awakens to find that he was previously in a made-up world known as the Matrix. All that he understood was really a mask covering the truth, meant to hold him and everyone else in bondage to a lie.

This is the plot from the movie *The Matrix*, made by the Wachowski brothers, but it reflects something else that is also real. There is a red pill of sorts that opens our eyes to a more vivid reality of the Kingdom of God. It is the truth of God's Word that we need in order to be set free and unleash the power of His Kingdom on this planet. The Scriptures have always held the truth, but our mind has been blinded by a warped sense of spiritual reality. This book could open our eyes to see the church, the Kingdom, and our role in both in a more vivid and real light.

Many people are longing for a greater cause. They are no longer content with "church as usual." They read of the church in the New Testament, and their curiosity is piqued. The New Testament accounts are far removed from their experience every week. They hear contemporary stories of the church expanding rapidly in parts of China and India, and their hearts soar. Dare they dream for something more? "Can I experience the same power?" they ask. "Can God work here, in this place? Will the Kingdom of God unleash itself on an unsuspecting society such as the United States?" Yes. *Yes!*

"Thy Kingdom come, Thy will be done, on earth as it is in heaven" (Matt. 6:10).

Before he swallowed the red pill in *The Matrix*, Neo was given another choice.

"Stop the car!" commands a member of the strange sect that has abducted him and taken him to meet Morpheus. She turns in the car to face Neo with a gun in her hand and demands that he surrender completely to their agenda or to take a walk. He responds with defiance. As he opens the door to leave, Trinity, a beautiful and respected computer hacker, stops him and tells him to trust her. He asks why he should trust someone he's just met.

Gazing down a dark street with rain pounding down relentlessly, she says, "Because you have been down there, Neo. You know that road. You know exactly where it ends. And I know that's not where you want to be."

Neo slowly gets back into the car, unknowingly resigned to an appointment with a red pill.

When you look at the conventional church in America and all that it offers, you are left gazing down an old soggy street. It does not compel you to go further down that road. More vision statements, more Christian concerts, more sermons, and more blueprints for bigger auditoriums are not enough.

You will be amazed what people do for Jesus that they will not do for your vision statement. There is something better. There has to be. Jesus did not die and rise from the dead so that we can have better church bulletins and more comfortable pews.

To adapt the words of a fictional prophet known, in *The Matrix*, only as Morpheus: "Let me tell you why you are here. You are here because you know something. What you know you can't explain.

But you feel it. You've felt it your entire life. That there's something wrong with the Church. You don't know what it is, but it's there, like a splinter in your mind driving you mad. It is this feeling that has brought you to this book. You know what I am talking about."

After reading this book, you may not want to go back. The ideas shared here have ruined people for the ordinary church. This is your last warning.

All around the world, people are taking the red pill, and they are not going back. Church, as you know it, will change. This is your moment of choice. This is your red pill.

The rabbit hole awaits. Let the adventure begin.

Introduction

Christianity has been buried inside the walls of
churches and secured with the shackles of
dogmatism. Let it be liberated to come into the
midst of us and teach us freedom, equality and love.

—*Minna Canth*

For many years now I have taken to going to
church less and less because I find so little there of
what I hunger for. It is a sense of the presence of
God that I hunger for.

—*Frederick Buechner*

"Houston, we have a problem."

This historic understatement was uttered on April 14, 1970, by
Cdr. James A. Lovell while floating aimlessly in a small metal capsule hundreds of miles from earth aboard *Apollo 13*. Something had
gone terribly wrong. Without enough oxygen or propulsion to get
home safely, the spaceship crew and the team of NASA experts in
Houston faced a great challenge. Well documented in dramatic
fashion by Ron Howard in the movie *Apollo 13*, this episode could
have become either a great tragedy or NASA's finest hour. The
statement echoing in space began the process of looking for creative
solutions to a complex challenge.

Today the Church can say something similar. "Heaven, we have
a problem."

The words in this book may not be something you want to hear,
any more than Houston wanted to hear those words. But if we are

not willing to face our problems, we will never be able to correct our path. It is a love for Jesus and His church, His bride, that has motivated this writing.

Modern pollsters tell us that a large number of those who are not Christians are indeed interested in Christ but not in attending church. One bumper sticker reads, "I love Jesus; it's Christians I can't stand."

I attended a meeting with several thousand pastors to view Mel Gibson's film *The Passion of the Christ* before its release to the public. The buzz at the meeting was that this movie was going to be very popular and cause multitudes of people to come back to church. Sermons reaching out to the seekers for this occasion were already written and available for download online. Slick and colorful advertisements were produced to draw the masses to our church services. Entire theaters were rented out to have private showings, assuming that the people that were invited would come to Christ and naturally want to join our churches.

The film took everyone by surprise and sold more tickets than anyone imagined, making more than $600 million in sales internationally. Perhaps even more surprising, our local churches never saw any increase in attendance.

This shows us that there are many people in the United States who want to hear and believe in the message of Jesus but are not interested in the institution of church as it is. This should be a clear and compelling warning to us all. We have a problem.

Apparently, the world is interested in Jesus; it is His wife (the Church is the bride of Christ) that they do not want to spend time with. Unfortunately, we have reduced the Gospel message so that it is inseparable from the institution of church. We tell people that they must take the bitter pill of "church" if they want to even hear about Jesus. Most would rather die of the disease than consume that medicine.

The local church has become so undesirable that many, even among the convinced, are rejecting it altogether. In his book *The Present Future: Six Tough Questions for the Church*, Reggie McNeal makes an alarming observation: "A growing number of people are leaving the institutional church for a new reason. They are not leaving because they have lost faith. They are leaving the church to preserve their faith."[1] These are strong words. Could it be that the "churched culture" indeed is spiritually toxic? We have a problem.

Church attendance, however, is not the barometer of how Christianity is doing. Ultimately, transformation is the product of the Gospel. It is not enough to fill our churches; we must transform our world. Society and culture should change if the church has been truly effective. Is the church reaching out and seeing lives changed by the Good News of the Kingdom of God? Surely the number of Christians will increase once this happens, but filling seats one day a week is not what the Kingdom is all about. We do Jesus an injustice by reducing His life and ministry to such a sad story as church attendance and membership rolls.

The measure of the Church's influence is found in society—on the streets, not in the pews.

We are not alone in this ecclesiastical descent. All around the world, wherever church follows the Western institutional pattern, its influence is in decline.

A short time ago, I was in Japan speaking in front of a church made up mostly of young Japanese people. My wife and I were the only Caucasians in the facility, perhaps in the entire city. I mentioned that the number of church members in Japan is less than 1 percent of the population of that country. They all nodded with a sigh that exposed their fatigue in light of this reality. I then mentioned that I had been there a few months earlier, and the percentage of church members was less than 1 percent then too; nothing had changed. Noting this lack of change, I asked, "What's wrong with you?" They laughed at the ridiculous expectation.

I went on and told them that I had been in Japan three years earlier and the percentage of Christians in Japan was less than 1 percent then. This time they did not laugh. I announced that ten years ago the percentage of believers in Japan was less than 1 percent. I then asked, "Do you know what the percentage of Christians in the population of Japan was one hundred years ago?" They were now near tears as I answered my own question: "Less than 1 percent." After a pause, I said, "There is something wrong with the way we are doing 'church' here in Japan." (At this point, I would like to comment that we Westerners are the ones who taught them how to do church.)

For Japan to be changed, Jesus will have to give the people something new and powerful. The same is true here in the United States. It is not the local church that will change the world; it is Jesus. Attendance on Sundays does not transform lives; Jesus within their hearts is what changes people.

The Church in the West has sacrificed so much of what she is supposed to be about that her relevance is lost to the lost. Parachurch organizations, such as seminaries, mission agencies, Christian counseling agencies, and evangelistic ministries, have risen to accomplish so much of what God intended the Church to do. She expects others to do evangelism, leadership development, and social care. We send the people with serious problems to professional counselors.

If you ask non-Christians why the local church is relevant, they will usually think of only two things: it is where you go to get married and buried (hitched and ditched), and many people are trying desperately to avoid both. Is this what Jesus bled and died for? Is this the best we can do with the power of the resurrection? We have a problem.

Whenever the local church does attempt to engage the world in evangelism, it most often employs a "y'all come" type of outreach. The church, in effect, throws some type of party and expects the world to come to it. Under the banner of reaching the unchurched, we spend much time thinking up ways to make this sacred hour on Sundays relevant to them so that they will want to come. Books, seminars, audiotapes, magazines, and Websites are devoted to finding ways to make the Sunday experience so impressive to lost people that they too will want our Jesus. Do we really think that they will actually be impressed by our performance and that this will lead them to want to be among the churched? Is making them churched a sufficient objective?

How far will we go to get people to come to our Sunday worship show? How much will we compromise to gain attendance? The most extreme example I have heard was a church in the Northwest that actually advertised it would pay people money if they came each week for a minimum of a month. They literally paid people just to attend their worship services! This example is not very subtle, but have we resorted to buying attendees with our professional music, messages, and drama? It seems to me that we have lost the plot somewhere along the "seeker-sensitive" path. We have a problem.

Why must people wake up early on Sunday, get dressed up, and drive to a specific location to sit in rows looking all morning at the back of some guy's head while a person they don't know talks to them about the latest prescription of three steps to a better life? Is this experience really supposed to change their lives forever?

A missionary family who has started organic churches in some of the most dangerous fields in the world once returned to the states for furlough. On the first Sunday back, they visited a large Baptist church that supported them. They arrived early in their best clothes because Dad was going to share in the service. As the mother and two kids were seated on the front row watching the lights and sound being checked and the instruments tuned, the oldest turned to her mother and asked, "Mom, are we going to see a show?" Their whole church experience was more like a family atmosphere in homes, and this church seemed totally foreign to these childlike eyes. I am convinced that most of us are too familiar with it to see how strange our customs really are.

It amazes me to consider how much effort and how many resources (time, money, and people) are expended for a single hour once a week. We have made church nothing more than a religious show that takes place on Sunday, and after it's done we all go home, until church starts again next week, same time, same place. Is this what the bride of Christ is?

The Great Commission says that we are to "go into all the world," but we've turned the whole thing around and made it "come to us and hear our message."

We expect people to come to church in order to come to Christ, and the people of the world want nothing to do with church. We are so obsessed with our own religious club that we actually identify those who do not have a relationship with Jesus as the unchurched. It is as though just joining us on Sundays for an hour and a half is enough to say they are "in." Salvation is not determined by your Sunday calendar or your smiling face in a church pictorial directory. We know this is true doctrinally, but nevertheless we still divide the populace into the churched and the unchurched, as though all they need so as to be right is to come to our organization. No wonder our message is convoluted. We have lost sight of our prime directive and substituted creation of more people who are like us, rather than like Jesus, in its place.

Instead of bringing people to church so that we can then bring them to Christ, let's bring Christ to people where they live. We may find that a new church will grow out of such an enterprise, a church that is more centered in life and the workplace, where the Gospel is supposed to make a difference. What will happen if we plant the seed of the Kingdom of God in the places where life happens and where society is formed? Is this not what Jesus intended for His Church?

What would it be like if churches emerged organically, like small spiritual families born out of the soil of lostness, because the seed of God's kingdom was planted there? These churches could reproduce just as all living and organic things do.

We have seen such churches meeting in restaurants, offices, homes, university campuses, high school facilities, and beaches. We've had churches meeting in bars, coffeehouses, parks, and locker rooms. One of our church networks has as its purpose statement "To have a church within walking distance of every person living in Las Vegas." Another claims, "Every Christian is a church planter, every home is a church, and every church building is a training center." This is a whole new way of seeing Christ's church, and it is happening today all across the Western world. I believe it is a contagious movement that will connect with the many people who are disengaged with the old conventional church but seeking Christ. We must take Christ into people's lives, and it must be in the context of relationships.

I saw an article in a denominational magazine highlighting the outreach idea of a local church. At Christmas time they sent their choir to the local mall to sing Christmas carols as a means to get the Gospel out. This was paraded as a successful outreach. No one was spoken to. No relationships were made. No one was able to ask a single question of the churched religious people standing there singing in strange robes. All that happened was that people heard songs sung that were already playing over the piped-in music throughout the mall. Like a flight attendant at the start of every flight, the choir was announcing important information of life-and-death significance to people who took no time to listen because they'd been inoculated to it. And the churched people are convinced that this was a great work for God? Come on! We have a problem.

If you want to win this world to Christ, you are going to have to sit in the smoking section. That is where lost people are found, and if you make them put their cigarette out to hear the message they will be thinking about only one thing: "When can I get another cigarette?"

The heart of our message is that God didn't expect us to come to Him in heaven. He came to us. He lived life on our terms and on our turf. He became incarnate. This is a theological word that is worth explaining. Incarnate means He was "in flesh" or "in a human body." When I order chili "con carne," I am ordering chili with meat, or flesh. Jesus was God incarnate. He was truth "fleshed out" for all to see. He "became flesh and we beheld His glory, glory as of the only Begotten, full of grace and truth" (John 1:14).

This is what the choir was singing about in the local mall as masses of people walked by without a second thought. When Jesus came, He didn't wear brightly colored robes and keep His distance, singing songs to the public. He came naked through a birth canal, just like the rest of us. He had to have someone change His diapers (or swaddling clothes, depending on which translation you read) and for a time could communicate only by crying, just like all other people since Adam and Eve. He was poor and lived among us. He got His hands dirty and served the people. Eventually, He even came to me somewhere in the twentieth century after his life, death, and resurrection. We need to let Him come to the lost today as well.

Jesus is still incarnate; we are now His feet, His hands, His eyes, and His mouth. We are the body of Christ. We are His temple, and His Spirit dwells within our flesh (1 Cor. 6:19). We are not deity, but Deity dwells in us, and I propose that this truth is such a dramatically life-altering reality that all should notice.

Several years ago, in his book *The Crisis in the University*, Sir Walter Moberly identified the failure of evangelicals to penetrate university campuses with the Gospel. To those who claimed to follow Christ, his indicting statement still has teeth: "If one-tenth of what you believe is true, you ought to be ten times as excited as you are."[2] This is the word of a non-Christian who has listened to our message and studied our behavior. It hurts because it is true. It should sting. We must begin to let the Word of Christ and the Spirit of God richly dwell within us so that His divine presence is noticeable. It was for this that Christ died.

Theologian Lesslie Newbigin rightly says, "The Church is sent into the world to continue that which He came to do, in the power of the same Spirit, reconciling people to God"[3] (John 20:19–23).

This book is a call to return to our roots. Let the Church be alive, organic, in the flesh. Let the Church be birthed in places where it is most needed. Let the Church be fruitful and multiply and fill the earth as Jesus intended, as He paid for.

With *Apollo 13*, a dedicated team of desperate men came together at NASA and faced a difficult problem. Using simple components already on board the space capsule, they found a creative solution to bring the astronauts home. What was quickly mounting to become the greatest tragedy of NASA's history instead became its most heroic moment. What would have happened if the people involved refused to recognize that a problem existed? Unless we recognize the problem, there is no creative energy to devote to solutions.

The beginning of any great accomplishment is recognizing the problem. This recognition combined with a clear objective and creative energy can accomplish much. God has already given us all we need. All we have to do is look at simple things once again, in another light. There are solutions right in front of us, if we only have eyes to see and ears to hear what the Spirit is saying to the churches. God is not silent, and He is not removed, but engaged and motivated. Ask, and you shall receive.

In reading this book, you may be surprised to find out how simple and straightforward the solutions are. Though practical, this book is not about a model of church as much as incarnating truth found in the Scriptures. If you expect how-to answers that are deep, complex, and centered in methodology, you will be disappointed. The answers are not found in our models, methods, and manmade systems but in the truth of God's Word and in being filled and led by the Spirit of God. I hope this book will shake you awake and get you back into listening once again to the old, familiar voice—that still, small voice of the Spirit—calling us to walk with Him yet again. Anything more complex than that is doomed to bring dysfunction and failure.

Heaven, we have a problem. Show us the solution and open our hearts to receive it.

Organic Church

Part One

ROOTS OF THE ORGANIC CHURCH

When I took biology in high school, we had to dissect a frog. Some of the girls were a bit squeamish, but the exercise helped us understand the creature from the inside out. Before we describe the potential vitality locked within the church, we must first open it up and discover what makes it tick.

Part One gives a foundation for understanding the church. We look at how Jesus Himself views church. In this part, we define church and discover what makes it so special. We also hear a true story of a journey into a Kingdom that starts with a seed, the smallest of all seeds, and grows to influence the world in a very short time.

1

RIDE OUT WITH ME!

Can the church stop its puny, hack dreams of trying
to "make a difference in the world" and start
dreaming God-sized dreams of making the world
different? Can the church invent and prevent,
redeem and redream, this postmodern future?
                    —*Leonard Sweet* (Soul Tsunami)

Nothing is impossible for the man who will not
listen to reason.
                    —*John Belushi* (in the film Animal House)

In the film *The Lord of the Rings*, Peter Jackson creates a beautiful
depiction of J.R.R. Tolkien's world of Middle Earth. This is a fictional place full of wizards, elves, dwarves, dragons, ogres, and goblins. There is also a race of simple, rural people who are very small;
they are known as Hobbits. Sauron, the dark lord of evil in this
world, centuries earlier created a ring of power that holds much of
his evil influence. The ring was lost and somehow found its way
into the possession of a hobbit named Frodo Baggins. *The Lord of
the Rings* is an epic story of a small band of characters from the free
peoples of Middle Earth who face enemies in staggering numbers
and overwhelming odds. They set out on a quest to destroy this ring
of power and thus defeat the growing influence of Sauron.

In the second movie, *The Two Towers*, we find that the good
guys join up with the nation of Rohan, who are world-renowned as

horsemen with agile and brave horses. They face the advances of an evil army of Goblins, bent on the total destruction of all the people.

They find themselves in the throne room of Theoden, king of Rohan. When the king comes to the realization that the enemy is on the move and bent on destroying his kingdom, he is faced with tough choices. The counsel is to "ride out and meet them." But the king is concerned for the welfare of his people. War is ugly and always accompanied by great loss. In the past, they found safety behind the walls of a fortified castle known as Helm's Deep. With his shepherd's heart and desire to protect those for whom he is responsible, Theoden announces, "I'll not risk open war with my people." Aragorn, a warrior with the true heart of a king, responds, "Open war is upon you whether you would risk it or not."

These are true words today. We face an encroaching evil that would destroy the world of men. Our enemy, Satan, is on the move and taking ground daily. Christian leaders, like Theoden, face a similar crisis and must make choices for the good of their people.

Theoden chose the mirage of safety in the fortress called Helm's Deep. From that decision on, the film portrays men losing ground to the advance of evil. Once in the fortress, the men feel a sense of security, but the walls are breached, so they retreat further to the keep. Eventually the throngs of the enemy seize the entire fortress except for a small room with a barricaded door.

With the pounding of a battering ram against this last door separating the men from their annihilation, in helplessness King Theoden cries out, "What can men do against such reckless hate?" Aragorn once again gives Theoden the answer he had brushed aside in earlier counsel: "Ride out with me."

With backs against the wall, no way out, and no hope of victory against an army of ten thousand, this suggestion now comes across as only a way to die in a blaze of glory. Theoden says, "Yes, for death and glory!" Aragorn corrects him: "For your people." Theoden responds with passion, "Let this be the hour when we draw swords together!" They mount up and charge the enemy on horseback, becoming the warriors they were always meant to be. They meet the enemy head on. As they plunge forward in reckless abandon, the enemy surprisingly falters at their boldness and stumbles back. At that moment, reinforcements return to assist, and in the end the battle is won. Evil is sent running, and victory belongs with the brave heroes who, against all odds, rode out to meet the enemy head on.

This is a parable for our churches today. Under the good intentions of well-meaning leaders, the church has fallen back on its heels in a defensive posture, seeking refuge in its own fortresses of buildings, programs, and "Christian" businesses, schools, and ministries. Trying to avoid the threat we were always meant to thwart, we have lost ground over and over again until at last we have nowhere left to go, surrounded by wickedness. We are now seen as an impotent and frightened group that hides from the world and the reality that faces us. We have allowed the enemy to take over the culture and society, and we complain from the safety of our fortified so-called Christian strongholds.

Who Is Jesus to You?

But this is not how Jesus intended His church to be. There are two times in which our Lord spoke of "church" directly. The first time Jesus mentioned the church was when He and His disciples went to Caesarea Philippi on a retreat together, as recorded in Matthew 16:13–20. Jesus gave the disciples a "pop quiz." There is a good reason teachers like to give pop quizzes: they truly reveal what you know.

The first question of the quiz was easy: "Who do people say that I am?" This one was fun for the disciples to answer. Every one jumped into the discussion, each with his own theory. It is always easy to talk about the mistakes of others. What the disciples didn't realize was that this was only a warm-up question.

The second question was the real test—the most important question anyone will ever answer. Jesus asked, "But who do *you* say that I am?" (emphasis mine) The scriptures don't tell us this, but I imagine it suddenly got *real* quiet. I can also picture all the glances that were so on fire with enthusiasm a moment earlier now falling slowly to the ground. This question is much harder to answer because it is personal; if you get it wrong, it is *you* who are at fault. This is one question you don't want to get wrong, because all of eternity hangs in the balance.

The weight of this question made the air thick with tension. I can imagine all the disciples slowly turning their heads in Peter's direction, just hoping he would speak up as he often did and get them all off the hook. Peter, probably uncomfortable with silence, was ready to oblige. In one special instant he lifted his voice with boldness and a sense of power and said, "Thou art the Christ, the Son of the living God."

Jesus must have smiled at that moment, and the tension instantly lifted. Peter must have felt a surge of pride (he would later need to be humbled). Jesus was then to give Peter a blessing that would touch his life, and ours, forever: "Blessed are you, Simon, Son of Jonah, because *you cheated on the test!*" (my paraphrase) "You got the answer from someone else. Flesh and blood did not reveal this to you, but My Father who is in heaven." In essence, we all cheat death and judgment by getting our answer from God and His Son. There is no other way. All of us need help from heaven if we are to know Jesus. We don't get there by having a high IQ or studying the right books. It isn't intelligence, family heritage, or nationality that gets us to heaven; it is the grace of God. Only if we accept His help can we truly know Jesus.

What I really want to focus on in discovering Jesus' understanding of His church is verse 18. I begin with setting the context because this is where Jesus began. It is the right place to begin when we talk of what the church truly is. Everything about church begins and ends with a single question: Who is Jesus to you? Jesus' statement about the church has a context that begins with God's grace revealing the identity of Jesus and ends with the work of Christ on the cross and His awesome resurrection three days later (Matt. 16:21). Even if we get everything else right but skip this important question, we are not truly the church. Church begins with Jesus: who He is and what He has done. It is all about Jesus, and if it begins to be about something else, then it stops being the church as Jesus meant it to be.

Before one speaks about starting or growing churches, one simply must wrestle with this question: "Who is Jesus to you?" You must also find the answer from your Father in heaven rather than a how-to book or a seminar workshop. Church is spiritual. There is a sense of mystery and revelation about it.

If in your answer to this question Jesus is the King of kings, then church will reflect that. If Jesus has all authority of heaven and earth and is always present, then church will be different. But if Jesus is docile, passive, and indifferent, your church will be as well.

I think one of our problems is that we forget to ask ourselves this question when we set out to start churches. The consequence is weak churches. We speak more about our church "style" and "model" than about the Lord of lords who reigns within it. We tell people why our church is different from or better than other churches in town, thinking they will be attracted to it, but instead they are uninterested. If only we return to our first love and let Jesus be our focus, then many will be drawn in. They will be compelled to gain Christ rather than attend a religious service.

Church According to Jesus

Jesus went on: "And I also say to you that you are Peter, and upon this rock I will build My church; and the gates of Hades shall not overpower it." In only one sentence, Jesus says more about how church should be than countless theologians say in a library full of volumes. There are five things I want you to see about the church according to Jesus.

Jesus Builds the Church

There are many books, tapes, seminars, and CDs made to help people build the church, but if *you* are building the church, it isn't the church. Jesus did not say, "And upon this rock *you* will build my church." Jesus, and only Jesus, builds the church. If we build a church that is based on a charismatic personality, an innovative methodology, or anything else, we have a church that is inferior to that which Jesus would build.

Jesus Owns the Church

Jesus bought the church with His own blood (Acts 20:28). He didn't promise that He "will build *your* church." The church belongs to Jesus. He is building *His* church.

I once heard a story about a contractor who built homes in a small town somewhere in Europe. He built most of the homes for the people who lived in the village and was a gifted carpenter. Unfortunately, he was never able to afford a home of his own. One day, the wealthiest man in town came to the contractor and asked him to build a house. He said, "I want you to build the finest house you are capable of, and I want you to spare no expense. I am going on a journey and when I return I hope that the house will be completed."

The contractor agreed to the job and was about to begin when a thought struck him: "This wealthy man already has a few houses. I do not have my own. I will use inferior material, do a quick and sloppy job on the house, make it look real nice, and charge him the full amount. That way I can pocket the leftover money and finally afford to buy my own house. It won't be much of a house, but at least it will be mine." This is what he did.

When the rich man returned he went to view the house and was very impressed. It looked beautiful from a distance. The wealthy man turned to the crooked contractor and said, "The house looks wonderful! I am so glad that you spared no expense, for I intend to give this home to a dear friend who deserves a house like this one." With that, he handed the keys over to the contractor and said, "Here is your new home, my friend." The contractor graciously received the keys to his new home, but his heart sank as he realized what he had done.

What kind of effort and quality of workmanship and materials would the man have put into the home if he had known it would be the place where he and his family would be living? The church is Jesus' building project, and He fully intends to live in it. If Jesus is at work building His church, it will be beautiful and solid. He doesn't do sloppy work. If our churches are falling apart and are not healthy, it is not because Jesus has done a poor job but because we have taken the task upon ourselves.

The Church Is Meant to Be Growing

You have surely passed by a building that is being constructed. If you went by the construction site a second time you surely did not find it to be smaller. When something is being built, it grows bigger, not smaller. Jesus is building His church, and it should be growing. The church is meant to grow. It should experience spiritual growth, and seeing new souls brought into the Kingdom of God is part of that.

This doesn't mean that every local church should keep getting bigger and bigger. Most warm-blooded living things grow to a point and then reproduce. This is how the body of Christ is to grow. The huge megachurches of this past century will be looked upon as an anomaly, not the norm, of our time in history.

The Church That Is Growing Will Face Opposition

Jesus said that we would face resistance as the church starts to grow. He identified the antagonism as what comes from Hades. Wherever the church is alive and growing, hell is opposing it.

One sign of a healthy church is that she faces hostility from hell. A preacher once said, "If you wake up in the morning and don't run into the enemy head on, then maybe you're going in the wrong direction." Ed Silvoso rightly points out that "the Bible doesn't say to ignore the devil and he will flee from you."[1] We must stand firm and resist the enemy.

In *Releasing Your Church's Potential*, Robert Logan and Tom Clegg said, "I believe that the enemy divides all people into two categories: those he can ignore and those he has to fight. I want to be one of those that he has to fight." He went on to quote a World War II bomber pilot: "If you're taking flak, you're over the target."[2]

The Church That Jesus Builds Is Unstoppable

The enemy we face is powerful. He has been around from the beginning of time and has been studying our strengths and weaknesses. His first attempt to destroy human life was against a perfect man and a perfect woman who were not hindered by a sinful nature and were part of a perfect environment—yet he succeeded. He has been perfecting his craft ever since. He knows each of our weaknesses and vulnerabilities. He has an army of soldiers at his command. He and all of his forces are invisible and supernatural, and they surround us. They have been watching us our whole lives.

When I picture our situation in this light, I begin to see church as a refuge or shelter. I see her as a fortress where we are defending the saints from the vicious wolf pack surrounding us and wanting to devour each of us. But this description of church does not fit the one given by Jesus in this verse (Matt. 16:18).

Jesus said that the gates of hell shall *not* prevail against His church. Most people have a gate at home. It dawned on me one day that a gate is not an offensive weapon. Notice that there is no two-week cooling-off period before one can purchase a gate. Police don't pack loaded gates. Terrorists don't hold victims "at gate point." We don't send weapons inspectors overseas to discover "gates of mass destruction." Dogs don't run loose with a little sign around their neck that reads "Beware of gate."

Gates are not a threat; they are defensive, and the gates Jesus was talking about aren't pearly ones—they're the gates *of hell!* The church is to be on offense, not defense. The church has been held hostage at gate point for far too long. It is time we stop being intimidated by a gate. It is time for the devil to be back on his heels rather than the church.

The church in the West, unfortunately, is usually in a defensive posture. Christians are notorious for being against other institutions. If this is not enough, we are often threatened by one another. Some of us don't feel comfortable unless we are on defense, as if being on offense is a sin. We are so defensive that it has become offensive.

Can you imagine what would happen if the Denver Broncos decided to bring only their defensive unit to play against the Green Bay Packers in the Super Bowl? No matter how well their defense plays, they can never win without scoring some points.

I was once playing chess with a ten-year-old boy. This was his first time playing the game; we were evenly matched. Near the end of the game, he had already lost his queen and I began to chase his king all over the board. He would move, then I would move—"Check." He would move, I would move—"Check." He'd move, I'd move—"Check." This went on for a while, and I began to wonder how this game would ever end. While I was daydreaming in my self-confidence, the boy was strategizing. He set a trap. When he sprang it, my queen was gone and *he* was in charge of the board. I instantly went from offense to defense. I would move; he would move—"Check." I'd move; he'd move—"Check." Bighearted as I am, I eventually let the boy win.

Like that boy, the church today needs to make a similar switch from defense to offense if we are to be all that Jesus intends.

A few years ago, I was going to France to conduct some leadership seminars for missionaries in Europe. Before traveling, I visited a party with some friends and family members to celebrate the birth of a new child. Dana and I were the only Christians at the party. A friend of ours there heard that we would be in Paris, and she began to urge us to go to the Rodin museum.

Auguste Rodin was a French impressionist sculptor. Though many do not recognize his name, most are familiar with his work. He created *The Thinker*. What you may not realize is that the Thinker was really a study he had done to sit on the top of his greatest masterpiece, the Gates of Hell. For years we have been wondering what it is that the Thinker is thinking about. No, he's not wondering where he left his clothes the night before. The Thinker is contemplating an eternity of judgment separated from God. He is Dante, conceiving of the Inferno.

My friend at the party began to describe the Gates of Hell for us. It is a tall, haunting work with seemingly countless figures writhing in passion, pain, and agony, sliding down into their judgment with the Thinker sitting above it all with a mood of regret and contemplation. Each figure has its own story and identity tied up with Dante's Inferno or some other mythological story. As my friend started to picture it and describe each figure's story, she got caught up in appreciation for it and said to us in amazement, "Oh, I could just stare at the Gates of Hell forever."

There was a long pause in the conversation as her words began to sink in. A few gave an uncomfortable chuckle as it dawned on them how significant her words truly were. All I could think of to say at that moment was, "Oh, I hope not."

This adequately sums up for us the cost of the church remaining in a passive, defensive posture. If we sit back in our fortress frightened by all that seems to threaten us, we let countless souls remain captive to the forces of hell. We need to turn from defense to offense and storm the gates to set the captives free. This is church according to Jesus.

When we went to Long Beach, California, to start a church, our first plan was to start a coffeehouse. God ruined our plans by suggesting to us that we go instead to the coffeehouses where lost people were already. We began to hang out at a local coffeehouse called the Coffee Tavern. There we met Sean.

One of our team recognized Sean because they were both involved with a band at the local college. Sean was an outstanding musician before drugs took everything from him. He later confided to me that the day we first found him he was waiting for his drug dealer to show up. He was obviously hurting. His clothes were dirty, his hair greasy, and he looked disheveled.

Sean had sold all of his instruments to feed his speed habit. He had lost all his jobs because he would often steal to buy more drugs. He was circling around the drain, about to go down for the last time.

We invited Sean to my home for church. I must admit I was surprised when he came, and even more surprised when he came back again, and again. Eventually he even began to smile and interact with us.

At our first baptism, he was there taking pictures, so I knew he was getting close to entering the family of God. I asked him if he wanted to get baptized and he said, "No, I haven't accepted Christ yet, but I will real soon." A couple of weeks later, I baptized Sean in the ocean.

After Sean was baptized, he celebrated by getting high on speed. He and I were in a weekly accountability relationship. Every week we would confess our sins to one another, and he was always confessing to surrendering to his addiction. He was already attending mandatory twelve-step groups because of a court order, and he already had mandatory drug testing, but to no avail. Discipleship and accountability didn't work, so we stepped it up and had him live with us for a short time. He stayed clean while he lived with my family, but as soon as he moved back home he fell again to the bondage. I didn't know what to do to end this, so I suggested a rehab center. He didn't like that idea and begged for another option. I said, "Well, there is one other radical option we could try."

He said, "Great; what is it?"

I said, "You and I get in the car right now and drive over and tell your drug dealer about Jesus." With a smile I added, "Maybe if your dealer gets saved it will cut off your source."

Sean smiled because he didn't know if he should take me seriously . . . *but I was dead serious*. I said, "Listen, Bro, there is a darkness in your life. How are we to get rid of darkness? Can we vacuum it up? Can we just sweep it aside? No, there is only one way to overcome darkness: light. Paul says in Romans 12, 'Do not be overcome by evil but overcome evil with good.'" Sean could see now that I was serious.

He replied, "Well, all right, but it won't go well if you're with me. Let me do it alone." Apparently I look more like a narcotics agent than a drug addict. I agreed but added that if by the next day he had not done it, we would do it together.

He found his dealer (not very hard for a drug addict) and shared the Gospel. You are probably imagining a sinister man as his dealer. It was a woman, a mother in fact. Drugs are an equal-opportunity employer. She lived next door to him in the ghetto and supplied drugs for the local kids.

From that point on, Sean never took any drugs. He was free. The power of the Gospel, received and also given to others, transformed his heart. It is the power of God for salvation to those who believe (Rom. 1:16), and by sharing the Gospel with those who are influencing him Sean internalized it and learned to believe it in a more substantive way. We are often so quick to search for other ways to help people that we overlook the most powerful: the simple message of Jesus internalized and shared with others.

Sean's dealer did not become a Christian that day, but her fourteen-year-old son did accept Christ, and Sean baptized him. Within a year or so, we heard that she did become a Christian after her son was taken from her and she was sent to jail. Eventually Sean led several of the boy's friends to Christ and baptized them. He started a new church in the neighborhood made up of young kids looking for something better for their lives. He still shepherds them and is always introducing me to young people who have come to Christ.

Sean came to church one night and announced that he had started a new church. It was meeting on Wednesday mornings at 3:00 A.M. in a supermarket parking lot in downtown Long Beach. Why would he start a church that meets at such a ridiculous hour and location? Sean was working as a security officer in the city of Long Beach. He found several people who committed to Christ but who worked at night and sleep during the day, so now there was a church available for them.

The Church is a vibrant, authentic expression of Jesus' love and truth in this dark world, and with Jesus at the helm she is unstoppable! We should not be running from drug dealers and darkness. If indeed we really are the light of the world, we should be running *toward* the darkness with the understanding that we cannot be overcome by darkness. We should take the light and jam it right down the throat of darkness.

My wife, Dana, is a schoolteacher. She used to work for a Christian school but in recent years chose to teach for the Los Angeles Unified School District in South Central L.A., Watts in particular. This is a notoriously bad part of town. In her first week of work there, she came home with a big smile and a glow on her face as if she were strangely fulfilled. She said these unforgettable words that still make me proud: "It is so much more fun to be light in the darkness than to be light in the light."

I suggest we all learn to have more fun!

Jesus said, "*You* are the light of the world" (Matt. 5:14). He didn't command us to shine. He didn't suggest that we be brighter. He said in effect, "You already do shine, you are a light—that is who you are!" He then added that a light is useless if it is placed under a pot or basket. A light should be placed on a lampstand so that it gives light to all the darkness surrounding it (Matt. 5:15).

Ordinarily, in the Greek language, a pronoun or subject would come later in a sentence, but Jesus placed *you* first. This would have caught everyone's attention. The pronoun *you* is in a place of odd emphasis, as if to say, "You—yes, YOU—are a light to the world." He is speaking to you—yes, YOU!

Our greatest significance is found in the darkness, not in the light. The smallest light will defeat the darkest of night. We were born to be warriors, born again to be chasing the darkness away. Like the riders of Rohan, we must remember who we are and ride out and meet the enemy. This is who we really are, what we were always meant to be. It is the cowardly group hiding behind fortresses with stained-glass windows that is the caricature.

Friends, open war is upon us. Ride out with me and meet the enemy. Let us set the captives free and send the enemy running with his tail between his legs.

Let this be the hour when we draw swords together!

2

AWAKENING TO A NEW KIND OF CHURCH

Risks are not to be evaluated in terms of the
probability of success, but in terms of the value of
the goal.

—*Ralph Winter*

There is a difference between knowing the path
and walking the path.

—*Morpheus, in the film* The Matrix

Before we examine the organic church and how it grows and multiplies to become a spontaneous multiplication movement, it is important to give you a big picture and a short history. In this chapter, I share our personal story to help you understand how we stumbled into a movement. I do not tell this story so that you can mimic our steps and attempt to clone our success; that is a dead end. Rather, I share our story so that you can find courage to discover your own. It will also give you a framework to understand the heart of the organic church movement. This chapter is the story of how God led a pastor of an ordinary church to discover a church multiplication movement.

A Tale of Two Steves

For eight years, I was pastor of a pretty normal church in the suburbs of Southern California. In that time, we worked at developing leaders to plant new churches, and we ended up planting three daughter churches. In the early years, I felt the ministry I had was just temporary and that I would be moving on. As the years passed, lives changed, leaders developed, and ministry prospered. I found myself more and more content there. I felt as if this was a great little church, and I could stay there for the long haul. Many times, I had the opportunity to leave but after consulting the Lord, I felt strongly in my heart that I was to stay.

Then I published a resource for developing leaders with my friend and coauthor Bob Logan.[1] As soon as the resource was done, I felt a release from my call to the church. Without warning, and in a time when I wasn't asking, the call seemed to evaporate, but I was not sure what new thing I was called to.

It was at this time, in the seventh year of my pastorate, that we started to feel some overt attack from the enemy. In the beginning it was seemingly simple things aimed at our property, but then the opposition built to a rather significant event.

Our five-acre church property was in a suburban area high in the foothills of a mountain in Alta Loma, but we were only using one acre. Surrounding property was also undeveloped, so our church was actually somewhat isolated and secluded.

First I discovered that kids were growing marijuana on our property. Then I kept finding used condoms cast aside in the parking lot as I came to the office in the morning. These things infuriated me. I knew it was just kids messing around. I felt sorry for them, angry with the enemy for having his way with them on our church property. Just the outrage of his bringing sin and abuse right onto our property bothered me. Our church decided it was a spiritual attack, so we started to pray fervently. This only enraged the enemy, which culminated in the worst event of all.

Many times, when I was at the church building alone, I would have a strange and seemingly dark thought come over me. I imagined finding that a young man had hung himself. I assumed this must not be right and brushed the thoughts aside. Then one Saturday morning I was at the office and noticed that the police and fire department vehicles were coming, though not in a hurry. I followed them out to the old oak tree at the back of the property, and there was the culmination of all the impressions I had received and brushed aside. A young man, handsome and seemingly in good shape, had hanged himself. He wore brand-new, expensive sneakers and had some cash in his pocket. I found out that his name was Steve, he was thirty years old, and he had had troubles with his young wife.

Drugs, sex, and death were brought to our church property, all in the course of a week. This was obviously not normal. It was war.

As I looked at this man's body, swaying still and lifeless, and remembered all the impressions I had received, it seemed that a few years of the Lord's leading mounted to this place. I knew that this was an important spiritual moment, so I prayed to myself, almost instinctively: "Lord, what was this man thinking when he jumped off this branch and landed in the next life?"

As I was soon to discover, this was a dangerous prayer. The Lord proceeded to answer my prayer immediately. Every area of my life began to face challenges from the people I love. The events all seemed to come one after another, like a set of waves crashing in on me within a period of a few weeks. The trials also seemed to expand throughout my relational circles concentrically.

First, my oldest and dearest friend went through a short season of depression and lashed out at me, describing me as a fake who really did not belong in ministry. Then a church member began spreading untrue stories about me to others in our church; worse yet, some long-time supporters believed them. A fellow pastor in my area questioned my character, calling, and competency in front of my peers. (Isn't it just like a pastor to alliterate the three points of his attack?) Then, for some strange reason, another pastor in my own denomination from the opposite side of the country flew to Arizona to accuse one of our church planters of being heretical, suggesting that he needed to leave our denomination. I immediately flew to Arizona in his defense and found that I was equally under suspicion. Then I began to feel abandoned as my coauthor started getting lots of opportunities for ministry because of our joint work, and I was seemingly left behind. It appeared that I was losing respect from my beloved friends, my church, my professional peers, my denomination, and the Kingdom at large. There was not one area of life where someone whom I should love like a brother or sister was not personally hurting me, whether intentionally or not.

In the midst of this, I received a call from another pastor in our area whom I rarely saw. I happened to be the moderator of our denominational district at the time. This pastor told me there had been many atrocious sins in our churches over the years, and that I, as the leader, needed to take full responsibility for them and fall on my knees to ask God for forgiveness and healing. Just what I needed to hear amid all these trials.

As I listened to his words, I felt he was probably right, so I fell on the floor face down and begged God to forgive my people for their sins.

That afternoon my mentor, Tom Julien, came to visit. He lives in another state, and we usually only connect by phone or at denominational meetings. In this case, he came to my office to see me personally. I didn't ask him to come; he just happened to be in the area. This is actually the only time Tom ever came to my church. It was a divine appointment for an important moment, and I am grateful for my mentor's sensitivity to his Lord.

He asked me how I was doing, and I started to recount the previous couple of weeks from hell. He was very interested and concerned, and he started to connect the dots for me. I was denied by my closest friend. I was betrayed by a close associate, questioned by my peers, labeled a false teacher by my own people, and then asked to bear their sins before God. I was experiencing, in a small way, the fellowship of Christ's suffering. This was a chance for me to understand some of what my Lord went through for me.

My mentor looked at me and said, "It sounds like you are being toughened up for something." I replied, "It feels like I'm being tenderized." Indeed, my heart was becoming increasingly tender. I felt tender to the sufferings of Christ. I felt tender to the people who seemed to be attacking me. I especially felt tender to the young people like Steve who felt they had no hope, were not loved by the people around them, and were about to jump off a branch with a noose around their neck.

Immediately following this revealing conversation with Tom, everything reversed. After seeing a doctor and being diagnosed with a chemically induced depression, my friend humbly apologized to me. Our relationship is stronger today than it ever has been. The church member was corrected, and the church recovered. The pastor who questioned my character and competence in front of my peers actually brought forward the proposal that led to my new position leading church planting efforts in our district, and he has been one of my strongest supporters since. The denomination responded to the label of heresy and asked the "heresy hunter" to cease and desist. All my relationships were restored to normal, but things within *me* had changed forever. I had a new sense of call to bring the hope of Christ to people who are broken, lost, and not wanting to live anymore.

Despite the hurt I received from people that I loved, I never felt that my Savior turned His back on me. Jesus was always there with me, no matter what others said or did. I never lost hope.

At this same time, God radically called another man named Steve. He was one of our elders and a plumber by trade. Like the other Steve, he was also about thirty years old. We used to have Steve give church announcements on Sundays because he always told corny jokes and was such a lively personality. One Sunday, however, he changed. He went up to the platform and said, "All the announcements you need are really in your bulletin, but turn with me to Revelation, chapters 5 and 6." He then proceeded to describe what heaven will be like. Where I once saw a plumber, suddenly I could see a pastor.

Two young men in their early thirties both shared the name Steve, one with no hope, the other with an internal sense of call and a passion to live out the life that Jesus had placed in him. From this experience I knew God had called me to bring the hope and life of Jesus to young, broken people like Steve to become people with a sense of purpose and passion for life abundantly . . . like Steve.

The Start of Something New

After a year of mentoring the second Steve and setting things in place for the church, my family and I were commissioned to start something new in Long Beach, California. We were sent to find and reach people like the first Steve who were in deep pain and had lost all hope. We were sent to give them a sense of hope and personal meaning similar to the second Steve's. We were sent to start new churches, which we called Awakening Chapels, among urban postmoderns.

Starting a single church was not an option for us; we would settle for nothing less than a church multiplication movement, and we would abandon all things, even successful ones that would hold us back from the goal. I have found there are many effective ministry methods that also hold back multiplication. Success, as defined by most of Christendom, is often counter to healthy reproduction. We were willing to abandon anything that would not multiply healthy disciples, leaders, churches, and movements. For this reason, we also started a new organization, called Church Multiplication Associates (CMA) to develop the resources to accomplish the mission.

We selected Long Beach because we were looking for three things: an urban center, an area with a large university system and many young people, and a location by the beach (for baptisms, of course).

We came with a few methods that had proven effective in reproducing disciples and a team of twelve radical Christians willing to try something new. A far greater asset was our desire to learn and hearts willing to listen to what the Spirit had to say. The churches that God started did not look like our plans, but as we followed the leading of the Lord of the harvest we discovered ways to start churches that were healthy and could reproduce. These new churches were small and met mostly in homes.

I never set out to start "house churches" and am always a little surprised when I am considered an authority on such. We do not call them house churches. Instead, we call them "organic churches," to emphasize the healthy life and the natural means of reproducing that we longed to see.

We avoid the *house church* label for a couple of reasons. First, the house church in the United States has a reputation in some circles for being composed of angry, nonconformist people who isolate themselves from everyone and are stockpiling weapons in the basement. This, of course, is not true of the vast majority, but the label does conjure up negative images.

A second reason we avoid the *house church* label is because Christ's church is not contained by any building, whether it has a steeple on the roof or a chimney. We have found churches meeting in a variety of strange places. Vacant lots, parks, and parking lots have all had churches meeting in them, but we do not call them "parking lot churches." I have heard of churches meeting in locker rooms, student unions, and businesses. One of our church planters started a work he calls "Jesus at the Pub"; it meets in a bar. I have even heard of a woman who had a heart for reaching out to women abused by men, so she ended up starting a church *in a strip club!* We are not about to start doing workshops about how to start "strip club churches"—even though we could probably get a lot of people to attend such a workshop. The hope is that the church will move out of the strip club, but I am not opposed to seeing the Kingdom of God influencing such a place.

We do not mandate that churches remain small and meet in homes; that would miss the point. We seek that churches be healthy and reproduce. The reason our churches tend to stay small is the dynamic life-changing property of a "band of brothers and sisters" who are actively on mission together. There is an innate quality to our expression of church that causes them to want to remain small, intimate, and involved on mission.

These new churches we saw starting were different from others we had been part of. They were the result of planting the seed of the Gospel in good soil and watching the church emerge more naturally, *organically.* These organic churches sprang up wherever the seed was planted: in coffeehouses, campuses, businesses, and homes.

We believe that church should happen wherever life happens. You shouldn't have to leave life to go to church.

Because we were approaching church as a living entity, organic in essence, we followed certain natural phases of development. The result was reproduction at all levels of church life: disciples, leaders, churches, and ultimately movements. In all of life, reproduction begins at the cellular level and eventually multiplies and morphs into more complex living entities. Life reproduces, and usually it develops from micro to macro. Our movement has developed in just such a manner.

As we discovered new things, we shared our learning with others, and soon organic churches were starting all over the United States and the world. It may seem as though we know something of what we are doing, but we didn't start with an ingenious plan. Rather, we learned from our mistakes as well as our accidental successes.

Our first plan was an original, one-of-a-kind idea to start a coffeehouse. Do you sense a little sarcasm there? We had the whole scenario worked out: who would bake muffins and pastries, who would brew coffee, who would play guitar and sing cool "Jesus songs" in the corner. We even had a space rented to turn into the business. Then the Lord stepped in and whispered in my ear: "Why start coffeehouses to attract lost people? Why not just go to the coffeehouses where they already are?"

That was a turning point for us. Our original strategy required us to "convert" people from the coffeehouses they already loved to our coffeehouse so that we could then convert some to Jesus. The Lord of the harvest, once again, had a better idea. This simple transitional lesson meant the difference between becoming just another attraction-oriented "y'all come to us" form of church to actually becoming a missional and incarnational church that goes to the lost. The implications have reverberated now to thirty-two states and twenty-three nations in just six years.

Most Christians today are trying to figure out how to bring lost people to Jesus. The key to starting churches that reproduce spontaneously is to bring Jesus to lost people. We're not interested in starting a regional church but rather in making Jesus available to a whole region.

For the first seven weeks that my family was in Long Beach, we were homeless. A couple we knew had a house they wanted to rent to us, so we packed up and prepared to move, only to find that the previous tenants had changed their mind about leaving, and so we found ourselves without a home. We stored all our earthly possessions at my office and slept on borrowed beds and couches or in motels. We were a traveling band of nomads, wandering in the wilderness with a dog, a cat, a bird, and three children. For two weeks we stayed in a motel, but we couldn't keep the pets there. They stayed in my office. So several times a day I would take my dog for a walk. I remember one night I took the dog to the top of Signal Hill, surrounded by the city of Long Beach. While the dog was sniffing every bush, I had a heated discussion with God. Why had we been dislodged from our home? I asked Him what He was trying to say to me, and He answered.

In that night I heard the city, and God's voice spoke to my heart. I heard wives and husbands screaming at each other. I heard dogs barking, cars screeching, sirens blaring, and guns shooting. I heard the things that Jesus hears when He listens to the city, and I began to weep. In that moment, the Lord broke my heart for the city and the people of the city enslaved to darkness. I begged God to set the captives free and establish His kingdom in Long Beach as it is in heaven.

After that the Lord opened up the original house we meant to come to, and we moved in. The new house was a back unit on an alley, but without a yard. We still had a dog, so each night I went on prayer walks with the dog (well, at least I was praying; I can't speak for the dog). I found a coffeehouse in my neighborhood that was full of young people who were there every night. I would pray for this place and the people I saw there each night as I walked the dog. I spent hours begging God for the souls of these young people. I began to hang out at this coffeehouse with several of the teammates who joined our work.

We played chess, checkers, or dominoes with the regulars who came to the coffeehouse, and we became part of the crowd. We would listen intently to people's stories and offer compassionate prayer for those who were hurting. We did not really preach at people, but they would often ask us about our spiritual lives. There must have been something attractive about our lives because many were drawn to discover more about Christ.

Before long my living room was filled with new life. Rather than move to a larger space, we sent small teams of two or three to other coffeehouses to start other churches.

A Movement Is Born

In our first year, we began ten new churches. In our second year, Church Multiplication Associates (CMA) started 18 churches. The next year, we added 52 new starts. The momentum was beyond our expectations. In 2002, we averaged two churches a week being started and had 106 starts. The following year, we saw around 200 starts in a single year. We estimate that close to 400 churches were started in 2004, but counting the churches has become a daunting task. At the time of this writing, there have been close to 800 churches started in thirty-two states and twenty-three nations around the world, in only six years.

These churches we were starting were small (averaging sixteen people) and simple. The term *simple church* began to gain popularity, because we valued a simple life of following our Lord and avoided many of the complexities of the conventional church. Complex things break down and do not get passed on, but simple things are strong and easily reproduced. Ordinary Christians were able to do the extraordinary work of starting and leading churches because the work was simple, the results powerful.

We started articulating this profound goal for CMA: "We want to lower the bar of how church is done and raise the bar of what it means to be a disciple." If church is simple enough that everyone can do it and is made up of people who take up their cross and follow Jesus at any cost, the result will be churches that empower the common Christian to do the uncommon works of God. Churches will become healthy, fertile, and reproductive.

The conventional church has become so complicated and difficult to pull off that only a rare person who is a professional can do it every week. Many people feel that to lower the bar of how church is done is close to blasphemous because the Church is Jesus' expression of the Kingdom on earth. Because church is not a once-a-week service but the people of God's family, what they have actually done is the opposite of their intention. When church is so complicated, its function is taken out of the hands of the common Christian and placed in the hands of a few talented professionals. This results in a passive church whose members come and act more like spectators than empowered agents of God's Kingdom.

The organic or simple church, more than any other, is best prepared to saturate a region because it is informal, relational, and mobile. Because it is not financially encumbered with overhead costs and is easily planted in a variety of settings, it also reproduces faster and spreads further. Organic church can be a decentralized approach to a region, nation, or people group and is not heavily dependent upon trained clergy.

CMA's mandate is clear and simple: to reproduce healthy disciples, leaders, churches, and movements to fill the earth with God's Kingdom. We have developed some very simple ways to release the power of multiplication at each of these levels of Kingdom life and growth. Saturating the globe with healthy and vital disciples is our mandate. It appears that God is fulfilling our deepest desires.

The smallest group in our movement is not the organic church but the Life Transformation Group (LTG). This is a group of two or three people who meet weekly to challenge one another to live an authentic spiritual life. Members of these non-coed groups have a high degree of accountability to one another in how they have walked with the Lord each week, which involves mutual confession of sins as well as reading a large volume of Scripture repetitively. LTGs are also missional, in that they actively pray for the souls of lost friends, family, associates, and neighbors. This is the context in which we multiply disciples, which must come before we multiply churches. Some of the thinking that undergirds this strategy is explained further in Chapter Seven.[2]

Multiplication growth starts small and with time builds momentum, until it is beyond control. We look forward to times when we are surprised by the Kingdom expansion.

One evening at one of my own churches, Michael (who paints houses for a living) asked me about the church we had on Gaviota Street in Long Beach. Gaviota is only a few blocks from where I lived at the time. I told him we didn't have any churches on Gaviota. He smiled and said, "Yes, you do." He told me he had been painting a house and noticed that cars started coming to the house across the street. People would pull out guitars, bongos, and Bibles and go into the house. He went over to introduce himself and mention that he had a church meeting in his home as well. When they saw him, they recognized him and said they were also a part of our network of churches. A church had started only a few blocks from my home, and I didn't even know about it. When I heard this story, I felt as though we had finally reached a goal of spontaneous reproduction; we were beginning to see things get out of control. We still have much to learn, but God seems to be showing us the way to release spontaneous multiplication.

A couple of us from one of our Awakening Chapels started a new church in an apartment complex in the barrio of East L.A. On a Saturday we went to the apartments to have a barbecue and baptize new believers. When we arrived, I was surprised to see one of our other church planters there. He was also surprised to see me. He lived on that same block and led a church that he had already started there in Spanish. Suddenly there were two churches on the block, one in Spanish and one in English. Could it be that we are now bumping into each other?

I went recently on a trip to Asia with Phil Helfer, one of the key leaders and cofounders of CMA. On our return flight we met a flight attendant who was expecting her first child. As we talked we found out that she had lived in Long Beach and was a Christian. What we didn't find out until a few weeks later is that she was a part of one of our churches. It blows my mind that in such a short time we are bumping into people in our movement all over the place— even at thirty-six thousand feet over the Pacific Ocean.

After five years, I drew out a family tree for Awakening Chapels. I was amazed at what can happen in a single church network in just five years. Here is what I discovered:

The start of sixty-eight organic churches in five states and five countries.

Five generations of churches, where we had a daughter church, granddaughter churches, great-granddaughter churches, and great-great-granddaughter churches.

Five additional networks were birthed from this one. Awakening is only one of more than ninety networks so far in our movement.

This book is the product of our listening and learning in the journey we have been pursuing. I start by uncovering what I believe to be the essence of church. It is important to understand key concepts and shift our understanding of church and the Kingdom of God. In the chapters that follow, we unfold the organic nature of the Kingdom and see how the church begins, continues, and reproduces in natural ways.

3

THE ZOMBIE BRIDE LIVES!

Christianity is not a theory or speculation, but a
life; not a philosophy of life, but a life and a living
process.

— *Samuel Taylor Coleridge*

The gospel says, "Go," but our church buildings say,
"Stay."
The gospel says, "Seek the lost," but our churches
say, "Let the lost seek the church."

— *Howard Snyder* (The Problem of Wineskins)

In the Bible, the prophet Joel wrote, "Your old men will dream dreams; your young men will see visions" (Joel 2:28). In 1991, while on my way to bed late one night (I had not lain down yet), I had a vision. I haven't had any visions since, only dreams. (I guess now even God thinks I'm old.) In a single moment, faster than I could imagine, all my sight was consumed with this picture. It was gone as fast as it came, yet the image was burned permanently in my memory.

The vision was of a bride lying down on a couch, so weak she couldn't even sit up. She was so sick that she looked dead, but she was still animated, barely. It was as if she were being supernaturally kept alive against all the rules of the natural world, like something from a B movie about zombies. Her skin was a pale green and practically falling from her face. Her gown was unraveling and gray with dust. Her hair was thinning and unkempt. But the amazing thing was that her face had a smile on it as though she were waiting to meet her groom at any moment.

There was a window to the right of the couch with a lace curtain. Suddenly the curtain blew into the room with a burst of sunlight. Then the vision was over.

I didn't really need any interpretation. I just knew that this was a picture of the Church in America today: sick, kept alive by a supernatural force, but believing she was quite healthy and ready to meet Jesus. The hope is that a breath of fresh air and light is coming soon.

This vision set my mind reeling with thoughts about the Church as the body and bride of Christ. I went downstairs and began writing my thoughts down on a pad of paper, and those notes became the first draft of organic church ideas. I didn't tell anyone about the vision for a long time. For one, I didn't feel safe in my own denomination speaking about such matters, but more than that I felt that the vision was for me, and I didn't want people to think that the work I was doing was based upon any vision I had seen for authority. I am more inclined to share it now that time has passed and the work has merit of its own. However, the diagnosis of the Church that the vision revealed is still quite real.

The Church seems to have lost her sense of identity. She has forgotten who she is meant to be. Carol Davis, my good friend and mentor, has described the Church as suffering memory loss, not from amnesia but rather from the slow decay of Alzheimer's disease. When a person has amnesia, he or she loses short-term memory but maintains a basic knowledge of identity and is able to function. But Alzheimer's disease slowly takes away any memory both of how to function and of basic identity. Victims often forget who they are and what their lives are all about. They forget who their loved ones are and can even believe that family members are enemies with a sinister plot to do them ill. Their minds become deceived; unlike with an amnesia victim, someone with Alzheimer's disease may not even realize that something is wrong. In many cases, even the personality changes. As the disease progresses, the body may even forget how to do natural functions such as eating, until eventually the patient dies of complications associated with malnutrition or something comparable.

The Church has suffered in much the same way. She no longer even remembers the basic truths about her own identity. The very things that are beloved and given for our care are considered untrustworthy. Like the bride in my vision, she is deluded into thinking she is well, when indeed she is deathly ill. The result of this condition is that the Church has lost her rightful personality and forgotten who her first love truly is (Rev. 2:4).

The most insidious thing about self-deception is that you don't know when you are deceived. If you knew that you had left your zipper wide open, you would fix the situation. People don't normally leave their fly open on purpose. They do so because they are unaware, and as soon as they become aware they remedy the problem quickly.

I once wanted to make this point in an over-the-top manner with some pastor friends. We were all guys and in a retreat environment, so I felt I could stretch them a bit at my own expense. I stood up to speak to them and intentionally left my fly open. I appointed a trusted friend to relieve me of my embarrassment by pointing out my problem in front of everyone. He let the drama draw out a little longer than I had hoped, smiling at me all the time. Finally, he mentioned that there was a draft in the room and I quickly responded by turning my back to the audience to zip up. I had also taped a sign on my back that said, "Kick me!" There was a strand of toilet paper trailing down my backside just to drive the point home. Everyone laughed, but the point was made. Self-deception is ugly to everyone except the deluded, because he or she doesn't know about it.

Unlike Alzheimer's disease, there is a cure for our struggle. We can regain our memory, but we need first to abandon the false identities that we have adopted as our own. Until we realize our delusion, we can never find the truth and be set free. We have to turn to the Great Physician and be healed.

There are several letters that were written to churches in biblical times by some prominent people. Paul, James, Peter, and John all wrote to churches in the New Testament, but there is one other person who wrote to some churches in the New Testament: Jesus. In Revelation 2 and 3, Jesus dictates seven letters to seven churches in Asia. These are profound letters that open our eyes to how Jesus would address the needs we have in His Church.

There is even a letter written to a church suffering from a deluded loss of identity. In it, Jesus not only describes a serious state of affairs for such a church but also offers a prescription for healing.

Jesus says to the Laodicean church, "You say, 'I am rich, and have become wealthy, and have need of nothing,' and you do not know that you are wretched and miserable and poor and blind and naked" (Rev. 3:17).

Jesus instructs this church to "be zealous and repent." Don't be slow to turn around; this is urgent. It is in this context that Jesus says these now-famous words, "Behold, I stand at the door and knock; if anyone hears my voice and opens the door, I will come in to him and will dine with him, and he with me" (Rev. 3:20). For a long time these words have been misapplied to evangelizing unbelievers when in fact Jesus is telling *His Church*, "Open up and let me in!"

He concludes His letter to the church in Laodicea by saying, "He who has an ear to hear, let him hear what the Spirit says to the churches" (Rev. 3:22). We would all do well to listen.

Six Myth-Debunking Truths About the Church

Here are six basic ideas from the Scripture about the Church that refute common caricatures.

The Church Is a Living Organism, Not a Static Institution

Just as God breathed life into mankind in the beginning of time (Gen. 2:7), He also breathed life into His Church in the beginning of a new age (John 21:21–23; Acts 2). The Church is alive; she is organic.

God's very first command given to humans had nothing to do with the fruit on a tree or tending to a garden. It was more basic and has been repeated and never repealed. In fact, even the wickedest of sinners has obeyed this command. God said, "Be fruitful and multiply and fill the earth" (Gen. 1:28; 9:1, 7). He has given this same command to the Church (Acts 1:8).

Most of the metaphors and explanations of the Kingdom of God and the Church in the New Testament use natural concepts for identification and description: the body, the bride, the branches, the field of wheat, the mustard seed, the family, the flock, leaven, salt, and light. When the New Testament uses a building as a metaphor of the Church, it is quick to add that it is made up of living stones (1 Pet. 2:5).

We would do much better as leaders in the Church to learn at the feet of the farmer rather than study with the CEO of a corporation. It is time we see that the Church starts in the fields, not in the barns (Prov. 24:27). We spend so much time building nice barns with padded pews, air-conditioned halls, and state-of-the-art sound systems, yet we have neglected the fields. We are as foolish as the farmer who builds a barn and then stands in the doorway calling all the crops to come in and make themselves at home. It is time for the Church to get her hands dirty in the soil of lost people's lives.

The Church Is So Much More Than a Building

At least four times in the Bible, the Scriptures come out and say plainly that God does not dwell in buildings made by human hands. The first dwelling place God designed for Himself was a mobile home (a tabernacle) because He wanted to be on the move with His people. David strove to build a more permanent home for God but was denied permission. Finally, David's son Solomon built the first Temple. At its inauguration, Solomon stood in the shadow of this great building and said, "But will God indeed dwell on the earth? Behold, heaven and the highest heaven cannot contain Thee, how much less this house which I have built!" (1 Kings 8:27)

Isaiah 66:1 declares clearly: "Thus says the Lord, 'Heaven is My throne, and the earth is My footstool. Where then is a house you can build for Me? And where is a place that I may rest?'"

Fast-forward to Acts 7, and we arrive on one of the most pivotal scenes in the history of the Kingdom of God. Stephen is found preaching the Gospel to a group of Jewish leaders under the shadow of another wondrous temple, this one built recently by King Herod to appease the Jews. He recounts most of the Old Testament Scriptures to an attentive audience, when finally he says, "the Most High does not dwell in houses made by human hands" (Acts 7:48). Then he quotes the very words mentioned above from Isaiah. He goes on to say in verse 51, "You men who are stiff-necked and uncircumcised in heart and ears are always resisting the Holy Spirit; you are doing just as your fathers did." Upon hearing this, the crowd became so agitated that they took up stones, with the blessing of Saul, and executed Stephen there on the spot. This began a movement orchestrated by God to decentralize His Church via persecution.

Fast-forward ten more chapters to Acts 17, and we find Saul, now called Paul, preaching before the stoic philosophers of Athens at Mars' Hill. This is a pagan audience, unfamiliar with much of the Old Testament. Nevertheless, in the shadow of a great temple that still stands today—the Parthenon on the Acropolis—he says, "The God who made the world and all things in it, since He is Lord of heaven and earth, does not dwell in temples made with human hands; nor is He served by human hands, as though He needed anything, since He Himself gives to all people life and breath and all things" (Acts 17:24, 25).

Jesus seemed to not have plans for buildings. One day He was walking in the shadow of Herod's beautiful temple, and the disciples were straining their necks, enamored by the magnificence of this building, thinking to themselves, "Surely God dwells here!" In Luke 13: 2 we read, "One of His disciples said to Him, 'Teacher, behold what wonderful stones and what wonderful buildings!'" Jesus wasn't impressed. In the next verse, he responded with a remarkable prophecy: "Do you see these great buildings? Not one stone shall be left upon another which will not be torn down." Sure enough, in

70 A.D. the Romans destroyed the temple to such an extent that no stone was left on top of another.

It is important to note that the early Church did not have any buildings for the first three hundred-plus years. My friend Thom Wolf instructs church planters today to place a three-hundred-year building plan in their church planting strategy. Citing the fact that the Church did not have a building until the fourth century and did quite well, he suggests that the first phase of the building project come after the completion of year three hundred! Let's put this in perspective. Three hundred years ago, the Pilgrims were just starting to come to America. Something changes in our approach when we knowingly put off even a suggestion of building for at least three hundred years. I was impressed that, despite incredible growth into the thousands, Rick Warren waited fifteen years before Saddleback Church bought land and started to erect its first building.[1] Imagine a plan that would go three hundred years before you start phase one of the building project. Of course, if you can wait three hundred years to start building projects, then you really don't need buildings at all. I suggest that if we could figure out how to do church without needing buildings, we would be better off.

Buildings are not wrong or immoral. It is not the buildings that are really the problem. Unfortunately, we often begin to function as though the church buildings are our life source. Though none of us would openly admit this, we do feel we need them. It is as though our church's life depends upon them. Many a church continues long after the soul of the church has departed because the building itself keeps them going. A building can become an artificial life support system that keeps a church alive even though it died long ago.

It's not hard to imagine eight gray-haired people meeting every Sunday in an old building worth a million dollars that could seat hundreds. They continue in the sacerdotal duties of church and then go home. The building sits empty for all the next week until the same eight people come again . . . same time, same place. This scene is played out all over the United States every week—a different street corner of a different city, but the same scene nonetheless.

Someone once said that we shape our buildings and then they shape us. It is not just the fact that buildings hold back our growth; they also hold back our understanding of the Kingdom of God. Our minds can be held captive behind four walls as easily as our actions are.

In fact, you don't even need a building to be bound to this thinking. Before we started CMA, my friend and coworker Paul Kaak described a time he visited India to personally see a church planting movement. In an attempt to avoid all the trappings of institutionalism, one of the movements he visited refused to own buildings. In fact, churches actually sign a contract declaring they will not own any property, and if they do they must leave the movement. This is pretty extreme, but I am sure they started this tradition for the right reasons.

However, we can have institutional minds even without walls, offices, and staff. This particular church in India often met outside and would roll out a rug where everyone met. One of the leaders recounted to Paul a time when after one of the services was completed the kids were all running around playing. One child happened to run across the rug where they met, and a parent grabbed him by the arm and sternly told him, "Stop running in church!" Our problem is not in bricks and mortar; it is in our minds.

The Church Is Not to Be Bound to a Single Location

One hot, dry day, Jesus had an interesting conversation with a Samaritan woman. When she discovered that He was indeed a prophet, she brought up one question that had occupied her thoughts all her life: "Our fathers worshipped in this mountain, and you people [the Jews] say that in Jerusalem is the place where men ought to worship." Jesus said to her, "Woman, believe Me, an hour is coming when neither in this mountain, nor in Jerusalem, shall you worship the Father. You worship that which you do not know; we worship that which we know, for salvation is from the Jews. But an hour is coming, and now is, when the true worshipers shall worship the Father in spirit and truth; for such people the Father seeks to be His worshipers" (John 4:20–24).

We are always asking the wrong question: *Where?* All along, the right question is—*Who?* Where you worship is nothing compared to who it is you worship. As Jesus instructs the woman (and us as well), the reality is not that we need to go and seek God in some special place; He has been seeking us right where we are, even at an old well outside a Samaritan village. We work to create what we call "seeker services" but all along the Bible tells us that "there is none who seeks God, . . . no not one" (Rom. 3:11, 12). A true seeker service is one that focuses on the Father who is *seeking* His worshipers in Spirit and in truth. He alone is the "Seeker," and we are His heart's desire.

The Church Is Much More Than a One-Hour Service Held One Day a Week

The only time *worship* and *service* are put together in Scripture has nothing to do with sound systems, pews, sermons, or worship bands. It is a twenty-four-hour-a-day, seven-day-a-week expression of Christ's life in us. In Romans 12:1 and 2, Paul writes that we are to present our own bodies to be His temple. He writes, "I urge you, brethren, by the mercies of God, to present your bodies as a living and holy sacrifice, acceptable to God, which is your spiritual service of worship. And do not be conformed to this world, but be transformed by the renewing of your mind, so that you may prove what the will of God is, that which is good and acceptable and perfect."

When you imagine the amount of resources, energy, and time invested in a service held only one day a week, it is remarkable. With all the importance placed on this event, you would expect there to be a lot of scriptural directives to make sure people get it right. But if you search all of the New Testament looking for the commands or injunctions having to do with this important weekly event, you will find them sadly missing. Instead you will find verses, chapters, and entire books that speak to how we are to live together as a spiritual family. You will find commands and injunctions to serve and worship, but not just one day a week. How is it that we have gone so far away from the pure and simple priorities of the Scriptures?

William Law was an eighteenth-century English writer and mystic who made a formative impression upon John Wesley and the Methodist church planting movement. He made this observation many years ago, which flew in the face of his contemporaries, just as it probably does today: "It is very observable that there is not one command in all the Gospel for public worship; and perhaps it is a duty that is least insisted upon in Scripture of any other. The frequent attendance at it is never so much as mentioned in all the New Testament, whereas that religion or devotion which is to govern the ordinary actions of our life is to be found in almost every verse of Scripture. Our blessed Savior and His Apostles are wholly taken up in doctrines that relate to common life."[2]

I have found that so many years of running church shows on Sunday mornings has imprinted upon our minds an understanding of church that is not necessarily biblical. We find it nearly impossible to even think about church without a Sunday morning service event, but this is not the biblical norm. When we read of church life, we read into the scriptural text this idea. Try reading your New Testament with new lenses. Try to imagine the New Testament church without a once-a-week service. In fact, there is much evidence that believers got together with their church families *daily*, not once a week—and the gathering had more to do with a meal together than with sanctimonious liturgy.

How did we ever get to the place where church was nothing more than a one-and-a-half-hour service on a single day of the week at a specific location? I assure you, in Jesus' eyes, the Church is much more than that! He doesn't limit His Church to a building, a location, or a time frame.

A young woman who grew up in small relational churches overseas as a daughter of a missionary couple returned to the states to go to college. Today she says that Sunday is the loneliest day of her week. She faithfully goes to a church service every Sunday, but she misses the close-knit spiritual family she once knew in another language and culture. She has joined the thousands of others who find Sunday church service to be an isolated and lonely experience. Her parents have now returned to the States as missionaries to their own people in the hope of bringing the church back to a healthy expression of a spiritual family.

The Kingdom of God Is Meant to Be Decentralized, But People Tend to Centralize

God has always intended for humankind to spread out and fill the earth with His glory. When Noah stepped off the ark, God gave him the original command yet again—twice ("Be fruitful and multiply and fill the earth"; Gen. 9:1, 7). As people so often do, Noah and his family tried to settle in one place, and they started a building project in direct disobedience to God's design. God had to force decentralization with the confusion of languages (Gen. 11:7–8). The issue was not whether the building was evil. The reason God had to intervene was to force obedience to His command to decentralize and fill the earth.

The Church has been given a command to spread out and fill the earth as well (Matt. 28:19–20; Acts 1:8). But like all people, the apostles struggled with the temptation to settle in one place and build. When Jesus revealed His true incarnate self to His inner circle of leadership at His transfiguration (Matt. 17:1–6), Peter's response was classic: "This is a good place to be; let me start a building project right now!" (my own paraphrase, of course). The Father rebuked Peter by telling him to be still and listen to Jesus' command—a rebuke that is still relevant to this day.

It seems mankind always wants to settle in a single location. We also tend to settle for lesser things as well.

Many consider the Jerusalem church to be the best model of a healthy church. I see some good examples in the early chapters of Acts, but I think the local churches of Antioch, Ephesus, or

Thessalonica constitute better models. Jesus commanded the first disciples in Acts 1:8 to spread out from Jerusalem until the ends of the earth are filled with the power of God. Instead, they all stayed in Jerusalem. Just as God forced decentralization in Genesis 11 with languages, He forced decentralization in Acts, this time with persecution (Acts 8:1). One irony of the Bible is that under persecution everyone from the Jerusalem church went out, except the "sent ones" who were given the command in the first place. "Apostles" literally means sent ones, and they were the only ones who didn't go when persecution struck the church—a sad irony indeed.

The Lord of the harvest had to raise up another set of apostles to finally get the job done (Acts 13:1–3). Nevertheless, by Acts 15 we still see the original sent ones in Jerusalem, where they gave their blessing to the new apostles.

By Acts 21, Paul returns to the Jerusalem church and finally the sent ones are gone. But look at this model church. Paul is taken aside and told in private that he shouldn't be there, that the church was overrun with legalists who would attack Paul if they saw him (Acts 21:20–26). Sure enough, he is attacked and arrested, and this church tries to have the author of half of the New Testament killed. If we disobey God's will (whether in outright defiance or more subtle neglect), the consequences are an unhealthy church with messed-up priorities.

By 70 A.D. this local church was dead and gone forever. The only lasting effects that it left behind were accidental moves of the Spirit in alternative ministry ventures with second-tier leaders and laypeople, such as what occurred in Samaria (Acts 8) and Antioch (Acts 11). These new works eventually spread to become healthier expressions of the Kingdom that would actually obey Jesus' original command to fill the earth. Churches such as those at Antioch, Thessalonica, and Ephesus became a better representation of what Jesus intended. These second- and third-generation churches were healthier, more reproductive, and more intentional about reaching the rest of the world with the Good News.

Can you imagine what it was like to be one of the twelve disciples following Christ around for three years? Every morning you would awaken wondering what incredible miracles you would see that day. What would you think when you drank wine that was water only a few minutes before but tasted better than wine aged for decades? How awesome to see Him heal a man born blind! What would you think when you saw Him feed well over five thousand people with only the contents of a schoolboy's lunchbox? Imagine eating fish that never swam, or warm, fresh-baked bread that was never in an oven. Imagine the feeling you would have when you saw Him walking across the sea, faster than a boat filled with twelve men (many professional fishermen) straining at the oars. You would have seen Him calm a storm with a single command or lay hands on an unclean leper, only to see him cleansed instantly. You would have even seen Him raise someone from the dead, well after rigor mortis and decay had set in.

Imagine, then, that one day He says to you, "I am going away, and it is good for you that I leave." What would you think? How would you respond? Would you, like Peter, try to correct Him? Being with Jesus was by far the best thing that ever happened to these guys. How can it possibly be better if Jesus leaves? He tells us, "But I tell you the truth, it is to your advantage that I go away; for if I do not go away, the Helper shall not come to you; but if I go, I will send Him to you. And He, when He comes, will convict the world concerning sin, and righteousness, and judgment" (John 16:7, 8).

When considering this statement by Jesus, we must ask three important questions to understand the significance of His plan.

First, before Jesus was born, where did people have to go to gain direct access to the Holy God of Israel? The answer was in the temple, in the Holy of Holies, and there only one man could enter one time every year.

Second, when Jesus was walking on the planet, where did people have to go to be in the presence of God? Wherever Jesus was, whether that was on the shores of Galilee, on a boat in it, or taking a midnight stroll across it.

Third and finally, after His death, burial, resurrection, ascension to heaven, and finally Pentecost, where do people need to go to be in the presence of Almighty God? Wherever His people are, they are in the presence of the Holy God (Matt. 28:20). This is the rich prize that came at the incredible cost of the cross. Jesus died so that those who believe can go everywhere with the power and presence of God. We can find God's presence with us in Southern California, but at the same time He is present with His children gathered in Chicago and Cairo, Belize and Beijing. Now the Kingdom of God can enter into every neighborhood and every nation *simultaneously*. In Jesus' mind, this truth is so valuable it was worth dying for. We should hold on to it with as much value and care.

Jesus' plan was to decentralize, and He paid a dear price to make it possible. We need to rediscover the power of a decentralized movement with power distributed to each part that can in turn generate new life. Jesus' plan was ingenious. Do not disregard it and opt for another plan. Take another look at what He did and what He has given us to do.

We Are Each God's Temple and Together We Are Also His Temple

The New Covenant, established by Jesus' own blood spilled as a sacrifice, was to release a decentralized nation of priests who would multiply and fill the earth with His presence. Ezekiel 37:26–28 says: "And I will make a covenant of peace with them; it will be an everlasting covenant with them. And I will place them and multiply them, and will set My sanctuary in their midst forever. My dwelling place also will be with them; and I will be their God, and they will be my people. And the nations will know that I am the Lord who sanctifies Israel, when My sanctuary is in their midst forever."

Jesus died a horrific death in order to retire the old system and establish a new one. He tore the veil between God and man from top to bottom, removing the separation of God from His people. He has established a new nation of priests (1 Pet. 2:8–9) to cover the globe with His power, His presence, and His glory.

Why, then, do we work so hard to reestablish the old ways with centralized buildings, priests, and constant offerings to appease the system?

God dwells in His people! We are His temple, all of us from the smallest to the biggest (1 Cor. 3:16; 6:19). Our hope of glory is not in the buildings we use but in the Master who is building His life in us. As Paul writes, "Christ in you [is] the hope of glory" (Col. 1:27). The world is not very impressed with our sacred houses of worship; in fact, other religions have built more beautiful ones. We must let them see something they cannot reproduce: a new life in Christ. A transformed soul . . . now, that is something that the world cannot accomplish and is dying to see!

Jesus paid a huge price to set His people free to take His presence everywhere. We need to resist the seductive magnet of glamorous buildings and religious hierarchical systems that bind us to a place and form of church that cannot spread His glory across the planet. Recognize, once again, the beauty of the New Covenant: a decentralized nation of priests bringing the presence of Christ all over the world. All of us who are children of God have been set free and empowered in order to spread His glory all over the place. We are not all called to go overseas, but we are all called to take His presence into the dark pockets of lost people in our world. Whether to your neighborhood or the nations, Christ in you is the hope of glory. Freely you have received; now freely give.

There is a new breath coming into the Church. Rays of light from God's Son are shining on His bride once more. There is hope, if we have ears to hear what the Spirit is saying.

4

A DANGEROUS QUESTION

To look at something as though we had never seen
it before requires great courage.

—*Henri Matisse*

Christendom has done away with Christianity
without quite being aware of it.

—*Søren Kierkegaard*

Early in our attempts at church planting, before we began starting
organic churches, I was called in to consult with a new church that
was struggling with leadership issues. I ended up interviewing a
good number of people in the church. The main issue was a desire
to have a constitution, bylaws, and qualified elders that would en-
able the church to be recognized by its particular denomination as
a real church. Apparently, many felt they were not a church until
they had those elements. The pastor, who had planted the church,
felt that other areas of growth and development were more important at the time and resigned over the conflict.

At one point, I needed a nice, quiet time alone with the Lord,
so I went out to lunch by myself. I sat down, asking the Lord one of
the most dangerous questions I have ever asked: "OK, Lord, so what
is a church anyway?"

There are some questions that take us on a journey of discovery.
They beg for more than a textbook answer or even complex explanation. This question lifted me up by the collar and dragged me
down a road I did not expect, to new lands I did not know existed.

It was a dangerous question, and I do not recommend it if you are not willing to pay the price. Nevertheless, I myself would not hesitate to take this journey again.

As I sat at the restaurant contemplating this query, a friendly waitress came up to take my order. As she was about to leave, I noticed that she was wearing a ring on her hand that had a fish symbol on it. I thought, "Isn't that just like the Lord to encourage me and address my concerns by sending a sister in the Lord to my table, and by showing me that the true Church is much more than these petty concerns over corporation structures and bylaws?"

The fish has been a symbol of Christ from the early days of the Church. It began when the Church was under horrendous persecution and was driven underground—literally, into the catacombs. During those days of intense persecution, the Christians began a tradition of drawing an arc in the dirt with a walking stick or their toe. If the other person drew a second arc opposite the first, completing a fish shape, then they both knew that they were Christians and that they could fellowship freely without fear of persecution. The fish sign is a mark used to identify believers even to this day.

I decided to ask this waitress about her faith when she returned. She came back to the table with my food, and I said to her, "I noticed that you have a fish symbol on your ring. Are you a Christian?"

She said, "No, I'm a Pisces."

Ouch! It wasn't what I expected, but the Lord did help to answer my concerns. The Church is not to be identified by bumper stickers or fish signs any more than by constitutions and bylaws. It isn't a steeple on the top of a building or a sign in the front that says "church" that identifies the true church of Jesus Christ. Jesus said it was our "love one for another" that would identify us as His disciples (John 13:35).

This experience sent me into a discovery process to find out what is Church according to Jesus. I sought to have all my traditional understandings sifted in the light of God's Word, separate from cultural bias, historical traditions, and my own experience. This chapter is a summary of my discoveries to date.

Asking the Right Questions

When it comes to church, most people are asking all the wrong questions (What church do you go to? How big is your church? Where is your church? What kind of music do you have at your church? What denomination is your church? Who is the pastor at your church?).

I remember coming to a district conference for my own denomination, as the person they had entrusted to start churches in our region. I stood before them with this dangerous question. I honestly asked (four years into my charge to plant churches), "What is church?"

It doesn't induce confidence when the one who is supposed to start churches doesn't even know what a church is. How ridiculous it would be to have a car manufacturer who doesn't know what a car is, or to have a pastry chef who asks what a pie is.

When I asked the question, however, it caused others to reflect and realize that they might not really know what church is either. Oh sure, we all know what our experience is. We all know what our traditions are. We speak as though we obviously know the answer to this question. But in reality, most of us never took a moment to ask the question. Rather than starting with the question of what church is, we start by asking how we can make it bigger, or better, or start more of them. As a result, we are trying to grow something without even knowing what it is.

The temptation is to define *church* according to our own experience. We think we know something because of familiarity. By defining *church* this way, we are assured that we are always right, but this is a cheap solution that perpetuates all our current problems. It is much more vital to look at the Scripture with honesty and courage as we try to define *church*. Once we ask the question, however, we must be ready to expect the unexpected.

While I was an impressionable seminary student, I was given a definition that was really more of a description. Church was explained as embodying these five characteristics:

1. A group of believers gathered together regularly . . .

2. That considers itself a church . . .

3. That has qualified elders present . . .

4. That regularly practices the ordinances of baptism and communion as well as church discipline . . .

5. And that has an agreed-on set of doctrinal beliefs.

These are all good qualities for any church to have. Most of our churches, in fact, would meet these standards, but I think that this list is missing something very important. I often ask groups what is missing from this description. After a few minutes of responses, I generally tell them what I think is missing if they haven't already found it.

Jesus is missing!

One of my most respected mentors, a theologian and career missionary, once told me that Jesus is assumed in the definition because it is *believers* who are gathered. My response was, "Why would you assume Jesus' presence but make sure that a qualified elder is present?"

This assumption betrays a problem in our churches, a serious one. The church is often more about what we bring to the table than what God does. I heard of a Korean pastor who made a tour of the United States and at the end of his visit summarized his observations by commenting, "It's amazing what you people can do without the Holy Spirit." I believe it was A. W. Tozer who once announced that if the Holy Spirit were removed from the churches in America on Saturday, most would go on the next day as if nothing had changed.

Recently, a young church planter asked me, "What is the one thing you would recommend to someone setting out to start a church?" My advice was, "Don't do anything until you are sure Jesus is with you. Like Moses, tell the Lord, 'I'm not going to take one step forward unless you go first.' And let that be true for the rest of your ministry! I recommend you put yourself in a precarious place where if God doesn't show up and deliver you, you're dead." I coun-seled him: "Be angry at the fact that the world can ignore Jesus without fear of consequence." We have done something wrong if the world can think so little of Jesus.

It is God's name that is at risk, not ours, and we are not respon-sible for protecting His reputation. He can handle that, by Himself, just fine.

When we were looking at reproducing our ministry of multi-plying organic churches in Japan, we met with five men, hand-selected for their obvious leadership, call, and understanding of or-ganic church. We had received a grant from an organization that paid for our transportation, meals, and hotels for six of us to facili-tate this new undertaking. I felt pressured to make sure we had a re-markable meeting, but as I sat down to come up with an agenda, I clearly felt the Lord saying, "I'll take care of that."

It was risky to show up with these dynamic Japanese leaders who do not have time to waste, at someone else's expense, and tell them, "Oh, by the way, I don't have an agenda." But this is exactly what we did. I started the meetings by saying, "It is hard for me to do this, but I think it is absolutely necessary. We will not have an agenda here. We will seek the Lord and wait until we know we have heard from Him, because it is important that this work be His, not ours."

So, after some brief introductions and a meal together, we set out in prayer. As we prayed, the Holy Spirit began to speak to us and our prayers became more and more impassioned. We began to confess the sins of the people of God in Japan over the decades. I felt com-pelled to pound the table in indignation over the fact that 99 per-cent of the Japanese people do not know Christ and go about their lives ignoring Him because the churches have not been effective change agents. Before I could move my fist, my friend Takeshi Takazawa was pounding the table, visibly angry at the fact that the Japanese people can go through life and not see the real Christ; in-stead, they are in bondage to ignorance and sin. We were all con-nected to one Spirit, and with one purpose we sought the Lord on behalf of the people of Japan. It was overwhelming. We were on the floor, weeping, begging God for the souls of Japan and not accepting anything less than a new breath of God on the people of this island nation.

We felt the heavens respond, and I am convinced that on that day a victory was won in the spiritual realm for the hearts and souls of the Japanese.

As the meetings went on, there was one highly spiritual moment when, all of a sudden, the men started speaking excitedly from their heart in Japanese. I am not sure if they even recognized the fact that the conversation had transitioned, but the three Westerners were very aware, and blessed. We quietly left the room with the meeting in good hands—the Holy Spirit's.

When we later recounted our time together, one of the things that impressed the Japanese leaders was the idea of meeting without any agenda other than to seek God. This might actually have been a breakthrough, in a controlled culture of hierarchical leadership structures where the leader is supposed to be "large and in charge."

I think every church movement should start like this. After spending three years personally training His disciples, Jesus told them to wait in the upper room behind closed doors and not even think of going out until the Helper came. Despite three years of personal night-and-day, seven-day-a-week training by Jesus, these men were not equipped for any ministry without the Holy Spirit. I believe we need to learn to sit still and wait for God before we launch out with our strategic plans and demographic studies.

As the world looks at our churches in the West, it sees only what people have done, and it is not impressed. We scheme, "What can we do to make our church more appealing to the people in our community?" This is, once again, the wrong question. Once the world begins to see Jesus in our midst, many more people will be attracted to our churches.

A better question is, "Where is Jesus at work in our midst?" Where do we see lives changing, and communities transforming simply by the power of the Gospel? Where do we see fathers restored to a life of holiness and responsibility? Where do we see daughters reconciling with fathers? Where do we see addicts who no longer live under the bondage of chemical dependency? Where are wealthy businessmen making restitution for past crimes that went unnoticed? These are the questions that lead you to the presence of God's Kingdom on earth, as it is in heaven.

If Jesus is missing in our understanding of church, He will likely be missing in our expression of church as well.

In Acts, chapter 1, all five of the qualities I have mentioned that make up a church according to my seminary's definition were present. Many scholars believe, however, that the true Church didn't really begin until chapter 2. What is the difference between the groups in chapter 1 and chapter 2 of Acts? God came upon them with the presence of the Holy Spirit filling the believers, and what a difference that made. Without Jesus in the very core of our understanding of church, we are no different from any other religious group, Kiwanis Club, or the Moose Lodge.

We have a saying in our movement: the church must be conceived in heaven before it is born on earth. It must first be a glimmer in our Father's eyes. Church is spiritual and must start in the spiritual realm first and foremost.

The heavenly ingredient is so much more significant than the earthly ones. In fact, the heavenly ingredient gives the earthly ingredients their significance. If we minimize or even eliminate the heavenly from our definition, we end up with a church that is more like a computer without a power source, or a body without a circulatory system—dead.

In our organic church movement we have come to understand church as this: the presence of Jesus among His people called out as a spiritual family to pursue His mission on this planet.

Granted, this is quite broad, but I like a broad definition of church. The Scriptures don't give a precise definition, so I'm not going to do what God has not done. I want something that captures what the Scriptures say about the Kingdom of God. In one of only two places where Jesus mentions church in the Gospels, He says,

"For where two or three have gathered together in My name, there I am in their midst" (Matt. 18:20). His presence must be an important element of church.

To a church that has lost sight of its true love, Jesus says these harsh words: "The One who walks among the lampstands, says this . . . remember from where you have fallen, and repent and do the deeds you did at first; or else I am coming to you and will remove your lampstand out of its place—unless you repent" (Rev. 2:1, 5). To a disobedient and unhealthy church, Jesus threatens to remove the lampstand (representing the church) from the presence of Jesus. The presence of Jesus is crucial to what church is. His presence is life; His absence is death. He is the most essential portion of who and what we are. He should be the most important thing about us and the most recognizable aspect that the world sees.

In many of the churches in the West, ministry is done *for* Jesus, but not *by* Jesus—and therein lies a *big* difference. If we evaluated our churches not by attendance or buildings but by how recognizable Jesus is in our midst, our influence would be more far-reaching and our strategies would be far more dynamic. Unfortunately, it is possible to do more and more of the things that make up the five traditional qualities of church but not demonstrate anything of the person or work of God in a neighborhood. But if we start our entire understanding of church with Christ's presence among us, then we will want to see something much more.

Imagine for a moment three of the most powerful and dynamic people you can think of in two thousand years of history. Nero, Napoleon, St. Francis, Abraham Lincoln, and Martin Luther King Jr., would be good examples. Now select one of them and ask yourself, "What difference would it make if this person were on my church leadership team?" Whether for good or bad, these leaders would affect your meetings, I guarantee it.

I read an article once that explained how Michael Jordan came to the Chicago Bulls basketball team because of a simple flip of a coin a year earlier. Would the Chicago Bulls of the 1990s who went on to win six NBA championships in eight years have been different if Jordan had not been on the team? Of course. Adding a single, powerful ingredient can make all the difference. Now I ask: How would your church be different if Jesus Himself was placed on your leadership team? Would that raise your expectations? I hope so.

Unfortunately, we look around the table at the faces present on our team and think that's it. We forget that God Almighty is also at the table. We set standards, goals, and expectations that we think these visible people around the table can accomplish without taking into account the fact that the most powerful Person in the universe is also on board.

As coach of the Bulls in the 1990s, Phil Jackson began building his team around his best player. Everyone else was evaluated by how they supported Jordan. Our churches should allow Jesus to be the best player on our team and set expectations accordingly.

Someone may say, "Well, *of course* we recognize Jesus is on board; it is assumed. We even pray about our decisions." But the real test is if you conduct ministry business expecting Jesus to carry the load—to carry the team. Or do you practice church as though Jesus doesn't need to do anything, and everything is done *for* Him instead of *by* Him? This would be like the Bulls having Jordan on the team and never passing him the ball! Like leaving Jordan on the end of the bench to happily cheer on the other team members and tell them how proud he is of them while they sweat it out on the court. Sadly, that is not far from the reality.

We need to take on the challenges of God's Kingdom with the confidence that Jesus Himself is on the team. What would you do differently if you had complete confidence that God was with you in your decisions? Is Jesus merely the owner or the coach, or is He also the most valuable player as well? It is time to pass the ball to Jesus and see what He can do. I guarantee that the opponent will fear your church if you do.

One of the most remarkable things of the church I am a part of is that people expect conversions and transformation of lives— *every week*. It isn't a surprise when others come to faith in Christ. I am often told about new churches starting after the fact. I would not trade this church experience for a church of thousands or tens of thousands.

People who visit us can feel the presence of Christ in our midst, and it affects them. I remember when we were first beginning our church and no one had visited us yet. We would spend much time singing and praying. Our prayers were focused and passionate, begging God for the souls of people we had met. We also shared openly whatever the Spirit laid on our hearts.

One of the teammates asked if we should change the way we do things when unbelievers started coming, because they might be embarrassed to see us pray so fervently for lost people by name. I thought for a moment and said, "No, I think we should keep it the same. I think that people should see who we really are. Besides," I said, "look at what Paul says to the Corinthians in 1 Corinthians 14:23–26": "Even so, if unbelievers or people who don't understand these things come into your meeting and hear everyone talking in an unknown language, they will think you are crazy. But if all of you are prophesying, and unbelievers or people who don't understand these things come into your meeting, they will be convicted of sin, and they will be condemned by what you say. As they listen, their secret thoughts will be laid bare, and they will fall down on their knees and worship God, declaring, 'God is really here among you.'"

The next week, we had our first visitor. Her name was Alicia, and she came at the invitation of one of the ladies on our team who met her at the coffeehouse where we were hanging out. Alicia was quiet all evening, saying nothing, until we were about to close in prayer. We were all surprised when she spoke up: "I have been to a lot of churches. The one I usually go to is really big, with lots of people. But here, at this church, I could tell that God was here."

The fact that she said almost verbatim what we had read in Scripture was strong affirmation. She saw a small band of brothers and sisters who were passionate about loving one another, worshiping God, and begging Him to intervene on behalf of the souls of friends that were lost in bondage to darkness. She could feel the presence of God in our small circle.

The next week she brought her best friend, Michelle. This new visitor did not say anything all evening either but stayed in the back listening and trembling. At the end we sang a song about the nails in Jesus' hands and feet, and she surrendered her life to Christ right then. She was our first conversion and was baptized a short time later.

This church also has a reputation of having its prayers answered in dramatic fashion. Every week we pray, and every week we hear reports of how the prayers of the previous week have already been answered. This is a powerful testimony to the lost people who visit. They recognize that Jesus is with us, and it either draws them to Him or terrifies them, or both. Jesus' presence is a reality to this spiritual family, and we expect that He will do something remarkable.

One night in church, some "tough" Hispanic gang members came and felt the presence of Christ. Without any human persuasion or guiding, Tito repented in tears and accepted Jesus on his own in front of the whole group—some tough guy! He said that everything was overwhelming, and he just had to give up. This was *before* we got to "the message." Or maybe the sweet fellowship and the worship of almighty God together in an intimate spiritual community praying for one another *is* the message.

Unfortunately, in most churches in the Western world the presence of the pastor is more noticeable than the presence of Jesus. Actually, it is the pastor's absence that is more noticeable. This phenomenon is so common that on any Sunday when the pastor is expected to be away, the attendance drops. People say they missed him when he returns. I fear that we feel the absence of the pastor more than the absence of the Spirit of Jesus. Perhaps it is time we tell Jesus that we miss Him at church too.

I close with a verse that has often been used in an evangelism context, but remember that it was to a church that Jesus said: "Behold, I stand at the door and knock; if anyone hears My voice and opens the door, I will come in to him and will dine with him, and he with Me" (Rev. 3:20).

He knocks still.

Part Two

THE ORGANIC NATURE OF
THE KINGDOM OF GOD

Jesus used organic metaphors to describe the Kingdom of God in ways we could understand. We must unlock the meaning of His parables in order to understand the properties of the Kingdom that cause it to spread in influence so as to transform the world.

Chapter four of the Gospel of Mark gives three key parables using a natural, agricultural theme to demonstrate the organic nature of the Kingdom. This part looks at the three parables that describe the organic nature of the Kingdom so that we can better understand how it starts, grows, and multiplies.

5

KINGDOM 101: YOU REAP WHAT YOU SOW . . . AND YOU EAT WHAT YOU REAP

> You Christians look after a document containing
> enough dynamite to blow all civilization to pieces,
> turn the world upside down, and bring peace to a
> battle-torn planet. But you treat it as though it is
> nothing more than a piece of good literature.
> —*Mohandas Gandhi*

> If Jesus were on earth you'd find him in a gay bar in
> San Francisco. He'd be with people suffering from
> AIDS. These are the new lepers. If you want to find
> out where Jesus would be hanging out, it'll always
> be with the lepers.
> —*Bono (of the band U2)*

A few years ago, I was talking with a pastor and wanted him to understand the organic nature of the Church. I asked him, "If you had a plot of land and wanted to grow a crop of corn on it, what would you do?"

He said, "Well, I would till the land and remove the weeds and rocks."

I said, "Good, then what?"

"I would add fertilizer if it was needed and make sure it got lots of good sunshine and water."

"Good; what else?"

"Well, I guess I would take out any weeds that grow up and chase away any pests that try to eat the crop."

"Fine," I said. "Anything else?"

He said, "I would reap a harvest."

I looked at him with a puzzled look and remarked, "All you would have is a pile of wet dirt!"

He had a quizzical expression on his face as his words were rewinding and replaying in his mind. Then, suddenly, a look of "Ah ha!" came over him, and he added, "Oh, and I would plant seeds."

Though we long for fresh fruit, many of our efforts at growing it leave us with nothing but mud because we have failed to plant the seed that brings life. It does not matter how good you are at fertilizing, watering, cultivating, and harvesting. If you do not plant the seed, you will never have a harvest—*never*. The farmer who skips this stage is a hungry fool on welfare. Kids may enjoy making mud pies, but none of us likes eating them.

The Bible says, "Do not be deceived, God is not mocked, for whatever a man sows that he will also reap" (Gal. 6:7). If a man sows corn seed, he will reap corn. If he sows cucumber seed, he will reap cucumbers. If he sows nothing, he will reap nothing . . . at least nothing but mud. It is that simple. If he sows the Word of God, he will reap the Kingdom of God.

In the movie *Second Hand Lions*, a boy is dropped off to stay with two of his cranky and eccentric Texan uncles whom he has never met before. His first impression isn't good. Living without TV, they like to entertain themselves by waiting for traveling salesmen and then shooting at them with shotguns. The boy's summer suddenly looks to be unusual, to say the least.

Eventually the boy learns of his uncles' wild and adventurous past, and they leave a positive mark on his life. He also has an influence on his uncles. He convinces them to actually see what the salesmen are selling before they shoot at them, and then they start buying things like disc-propelling machines to shoot skeet instead of cars. They buy a retired (and tired) lion from a local circus (thus the name of the movie) in the hopes of having a hunt once again, only to find the lion is actually quite tame. They are also convinced by one salesman to buy a variety of seed packages to start a vegetable garden on their land.

Later, as the crops start to grow, they are out in the garden hoeing and tending to the emerging plants when a revelation occurs.

The younger and gentler uncle remarks, "Think how good all these vegetables are going to taste. Peas, beans, squash, tomatoes."

As he is speaking, the boy looks down at the row of plants he is tending. It has a stake at the end with the old package of seeds on top, complete with a picture of the particular vegetable it is to produce.

"What's this row?"

"Beets," comes the reply.

He looks down quizzically, noticing that this row and the others seem to have plants that look the same. The camera pans across the small garden to reveal the shocking truth that all the rows contain identical plants.

"And what about this row?"

"Potatoes."

"Potatoes?" asks the other uncle, also recognizing that each row looks the same.

"Yeah."

"Wait one minute here. What's this row here?"

"Tomatoes."

"Tomatoes?"

"Yeah."

The gruff, older uncle starts walking down the rows of stakes reading each label.

"That's lettuce, squash, sweet potatoes, carrots, bok choy. Bok choy? What's that?"

"Chinese cabbage."

The boy says, "Hey, that row looks right," as he points to a row with a corn seed package on the stake.

"Yeah, well, that's 'cause it's corn," says the older uncle.

"All those seeds did look alike, come to think of it," concedes the younger uncle.

"Yeah, like corn."

"Boy, that seed salesman sure saw us coming."

"No," retorts the older uncle, "saw *you* coming. Corn, corn, corn! Nothing but corn. Corn. Corn!"

Later in the film they reap the harvest of their hard work, and we see the three of them enjoying a nice dinner with plenty of food . . . *all corn.*

Don't believe the promise of every package you can buy to make your ministry grow and your life become more fruitful. Packages lie. Seeds tell the truth. You reap what you sow. There is another indisputable law in the natural world: not only do you reap what you sow, but also you eat what you reap. Fruit pies taste much better than mud pies.

The Gospel of Mark, chapter 4, gives us a remarkable look at how Jesus views His own Kingdom. The first thing we notice is that it is *organic* in nature. Three parables in a row are all agricultural and organic, and all are foundational to understanding the Kingdom of God. In this chapter, we look at the first parable, and in the next two chapters we examine the other two.

The Parable of Where It All Starts

Jesus tells us that a sower goes out to sow seed. The seed is interpreted by Christ to be the word of God. There are four types of soil where the seed falls. The first is hard ground; it does not receive the message. The next three all receive the message, but of the three only the last one bears fruit.

Some call this the parable of the sower. Getting a little closer to the meaning, others call it the parable of the soils. I like to call this the parable of where it all starts, because it is the parable that Jesus says is foundational to understanding all other parables. He says in verse 13, "Do you not understand this parable? Then how will you understand all the parables?" If you have a desire to understand Jesus' teachings, you must first comprehend the significance of this one parable; all else flows from this truth. I firmly believe that much of what is unhealthy and dysfunctional about our churches in these days can be rooted in poor understanding and application of *this parable.* It is that important. Why?

This truth is the beginning. The Kingdom of God is conceived with the planting of the seed. If you get the start wrong, all that follows is wrong as well. When it comes to serving the King, our expectations, strategy, hope, and faith are all affected if we do not understand the truth of this parable.

Jesus starts by saying, "Listen and understand!" (Mark 4:3). The story is repeated in three of the four Gospels. Jesus gives us a clear interpretation of every part because this is so important that He doesn't want us to miss *any* of it. Have you ever given considerable time to reflecting on the meaning of this story? Have you ever asked yourself what difference this parable makes in your church or ministry? If not, you have skipped the basic math, jumped straight to calculus, and do not really understand the foundation. It is time for us to take a good look at this pivotal passage of Scripture and digest its meaning and implication for our lives.

So often we skip these foundational phases of life and expect good results at the end, and we are disappointed. Jesus shows us that we must start well if we want to finish well. Remember that if you skip the part of planting seeds, all you have left is a field of mud. If we are deceived into thinking that simply getting people to sit in an auditorium one morning a week for an hour is what it takes to start a church, we have completely missed the significance of this parable, and God's Kingdom is not being planted.

There are two important concepts related in this parable that must be understood. To plant the Kingdom and see it grow and bear fruit, two things are absolutely necessary: good seed and good soil. If the two come together, the results are great fruitfulness. This simple formula is God-given; it is true every time. It is a natural law of the universe that cannot be wrong. Bank on it.

Good Seed

Planting the right seed in the right soil is not optional; it is mandatory in order for the Kingdom to grow naturally. If the desired outcome is to grow apple trees and harvest apples, you will never succeed by planting watermelon seeds. Seed substitutes will not work. The correct genetic code is necessary for the life to occur and develop properly.

The Sower sows the seed. The seed is the Word of God (Mark 4:14). We must remember that it is God's message that changes lives. Too often we lose sight of this important truth. We believe it, but we don't obey it. Instead we plant a seed substitute.

We might not really give people the pure Word of God. Rather, we give them well-meaning messages *about* the Word of God. For example, I received Christ by reading a tract. After that, I was discipled with a fill-in-the-blank booklet that had me look at verses of the Bible, but not really read the Bible itself. I was then trained to use the same tools with others, thus perpetuating the problem. Later, I went off to seminary, where I studied many books about the Bible, but rarely the Bible itself. Eventually, I became a pastor who developed his own curriculum and gave that to people. Many would come on Sundays to hear me preach God's Word, but they didn't receive the seed; they received a message about the seed—a seed substitute.

Many of us have a thick and heavy study Bible, sometimes with some famous preacher's name on it, as though he wrote the book. When you open it up, it turns out he did write it—at least half of it. It used to be that if you opened your Bible right in the middle you would be in Psalms. Today with these study Bibles, it flops open to Leviticus! The pages are full of notes explaining every verse for us so that we understand it better. Literally half of every page is notes that are not God's Word. Does this really help us? Are we telling people that God's Word is too complicated for ordinary folk?

Do we really think we can improve upon God's Word? Why do we so often give people our own teachings and curriculum rather than Jesus' teaching? Are we so arrogant that we think our own messages are better than God's? Do we really believe that God's Word needs our help?

The helps that are available to us are not sinister or wrong, but they are also not the seed of God's Kingdom. As helpful as they can be at supplementing our understanding, they can also supplant the Word if we become more dependent on them than on the Scriptures themselves. This dependency can be dangerous for the life of

God's Kingdom, by making the Scriptures appear too challenging for ordinary Christians to read or interpret.

When I consider the cost of so many lives that were spent in the struggle to give free access to God's Word, I am ashamed at how we have neglected it. As long as we read books about the Bible and not the Bible itself, the enemy has succeeded in keeping the Kingdom sterile, unhealthy, and weak. He has snatched the seed away before it can ever penetrate our hearts and grow to life and fruitfulness.

There is no substitute for God's Word; it alone is the seed of His Kingdom. Seedless watermelons may be convenient, but if that is all we produce then soon our children and grandchildren will not know the sweet taste of a cold, juicy watermelon slice at a summer barbecue.

I have heard people say, "Oh I try to read the Bible, but it is confusing. But when I hear you teach the Word, it comes alive, and I understand it so much more." To the boastful pride of the flesh, this sounds great, but in a spiritual dimension it is grievous. Do not be complimented by such a statement; instead, be saddened. Think of all the lives that were sacrificed so that this person can have the Scriptures, only to find them not enough.

Many Western Christians have been deluded into thinking that a verse a day keeps the devil away. For many, their entire intake of God's Word consists of reading a daily verse off a calendar and listening to a Biblical sermon once a week. We should not wonder why the Kingdom is not growing in the West. Jesus' parable describes abundant sowing of the seed, seemingly indiscriminant of where it lands. To see the life of the Kingdom germinate, grow, and bear fruit, God's Word must be received abundantly and it must penetrate deeply into our souls. If you do not plant the seed, you will not grow the life and see the fruit. It is that simple.

In my training, I recommend that people read entire books of the Bible repetitively as a regular discipline. Our Life Transformation Groups (LTGs) involve this in a simple strategy that anyone can do. In LTGs we read around thirty chapters of the Bible each week. I often get initial resistance to so much reading. (You might or might not be surprised to hear that those who protest the loudest are pastors.) If we have become too busy in ministry for God's Word, we need to repent!

Understand that it is not religious reading of the Bible that is important, but hearing God's voice. The Scriptures are alive with God's voice, and the Holy Spirit in us is a special anointing that gives each of us direct access to God's heart every time we open the Word.

Good Soil

The four soils in the parable represent four kinds of people and the effect that the message of God has on them.

The first soil, Jesus tells us, is hard and unreceptive. The seed never penetrates the soil's hard exterior, and the seed is wasted; it is "for the birds." We all know people like this. They never really give any attention to the message of God. They don't even hear what you tell them, and the enemy takes all hope away. They want nothing to do with the Kingdom, and even what little they are told is taken away quickly by the enemy.

The second soil is shallow. This represents a person who initially receives the message with great joy. The life germinates and begins to grow. But the soil is shallow, without any real depth to sustain the choice the person has made. When the heat of persecution arises, or even the troubles of an ordinary life, the person responds with fear. In her eyes, the choice she made was merely to make life better and persecution and trials are not part of what she was looking for. The result is that she quickly gives up on the choice and goes looking for something else that gives the false hope of a life that is easier. We all know people like this; they fold under pressure because their commitment is shallow.

The third soil that Jesus mentions is thorn-infested. This refers to a person who gladly receives the Gospel, which germinates and becomes a life that grows quickly. Unfortunately, this person is more interested in the riches of the world and the worries that accompany such pursuits. The weeds of worry and a desire for finer things choke this life that could bear fruit. We all know people like this. They are Christians, but their true commitment is to a life of comfort more than a life of service. These people will say the right things when asked about Christ, but their own desires rule their lives, not the person of Jesus.

The fourth soil is the good soil. This soil portrays the people who receive the seed of God's Word and in them it grows and bears fruit, some thirtyfold, some sixtyfold, and some a hundredfold.

One might find this parable discouraging, as only one out of four soils actually bears fruit. I find it encouraging and life-affirming, because it reflects my true experience. I have now come to expect two-thirds of those who accept the message of the Kingdom to fizzle out and not bear fruit. This has given me hope. Why? Because I no longer feel responsible for the fruit, or lack thereof, in the lives of disciples.

If ten people accept the Gospel and only two bear fruit, I no longer babysit the unfruitful eight. Instead, I invest my life in the two. These two will bear much fruit.

I am convinced that we have made a serious mistake by accommodating bad soil in our churches. When we see people come to Christ and then slip away, we assume a responsibility that is not ours. We would not take it on if we truly listened to this parable. We assume that we must be doing something wrong if so many people fall away from following Christ. We then doubt our ministry efforts and search for other ways to keep people. The results are devastating to the local church.

Because we think that the number of people is a sure sign of fruitfulness and success, we do everything we can to keep people. We try to woo people to come and keep coming. What we end up with is an audience of consumers shopping for the best "services." We cater to this sort of thinking by trying to compete with other churches with a better show.

We compromise the life of the church if we keep bad soil in our membership. We make church a show that requires the audience to make little or no effort. If someone is willing to come to our service once a week for a little more than an hour and sit passively watching others do the work, then they are considered members in good standing, no matter what the rest of their week is like. One can be totally uncommitted to the Kingdom, distracted by the deceitfulness of riches and the desire for other things, and still be a member of our church, complete with a smiling photo in our church directory. I have actually heard a person say he decided to leave one church family and attend another church on Sundays because the potential business contacts are better there. What are the motives of someone who selects a church on the basis of such things?

In his book *The Scandal of the Evangelical Conscience*, Ronald J. Sider looks into moral subjects such as materialism, divorce, sexual immorality, and racism and concludes that Western Christendom is only slightly better in some categories than the unbelieving world and even worse in others. Citing several national pollsters, he reveals for us that in America there is virtually no moral difference between those who attend church on Sundays and those who do not.[1]

Our churches are full of bad, unfruitful soil. A common refrain of pastors is that 80 percent of the work in church is done by 20 percent of the people. Reread this parable and you will understand why in a new light.

Jesus tells us that those who are good soil will bear fruit thirtyfold, sixtyfold, or a hundredfold. This equates to 3,000 percent, 6,000 percent, or 10,000 percent. That is much fruitfulness. Imagine I had a stock tip that was guaranteed to yield a minimum of 3,000 percent return but could possibly yield a 10,000 percent return. Most people are happy with a 10 percent return on an investment. Twenty percent is great. One hundred percent return on an investment is through the roof. How much would you be willing to invest in a stock that has a guaranteed minimum return of 3,000 percent? Even a fool would know to invest everything in such a promising enterprise. We must invest everything in the few who will bear fruit. Life is too short and the potential yields are too great to spend our lives babysitting fruitless people.

This paradigm shift will change the way you do ministry. We must regain the lost art of wiping the dust (bad soil) off our feet. We might consider such a thing as unloving, but this is what Jesus did. Perhaps it is indeed the most loving thing we can do. People must be confronted by the consequences of their choices if they are to get to the heart of their need for Christ. To do otherwise is not more loving; it is cruel, selfish, and counterproductive.

Jesus is the Good Shepherd who lays His life down for the sheep. He will leave the ninety-nine in search of the one lamb who is lost. Nevertheless, He would never force Himself upon those who are not interested, nor cater His message and ministry to trying to hold on to those who are more interested in other things. Although most churches today would be enamored if a young and wealthy leader came seeking salvation, Jesus was not (Mark 10:17–31). He gave the man some things to chew on and sent him on his way dejected. The Scripture points out specifically that Jesus really loved the man. In other words, this was the most loving thing he could offer the man (Mark 10:21–22).

I remember trying to disciple a young man who was addicted to methamphetamines. He would simply not quit, no matter how great the accountability. In one conversation I actually said to him, "Sean, perhaps you are just not good soil; perhaps you are incapable of bearing fruit, and we should both find something better to do with our time." Was he offended? Perhaps, but it certainly planted a thought, even a fear, deep in his soul. He thought about the consequences and decided he would not be bad soil; he truly repented. Today, he is alive, off drugs, and bearing much fruit.

I also remember saying a similar thing to a young man I had been meeting with for two years; in that time I had not seen even a hint of his wanting to follow God's voice. He was hurt and offended by my remarks. It is now three years later. In that time he married, had two kids, got divorced, and was served a restraining order by his former wife. He admits that my time with him was no more helpful than the drugs he was on. I am glad that I spent the last four years investing in others who are bearing fruit and willing to follow God's voice. It would be less than loving toward the others if I had no time for them because I was investing so much on someone who didn't want to change but was more than willing to continue meeting with me. He and I are still cordial and friendly, but I am not about to spend time with him until I see a change of heart. This would not be the loving thing to do for him or for the many other people I spend time with.

I've heard it said that life is like a coin: you can spend it any way you want, but you can only spend it once. Life is too short and God's Word is too precious to waste.

I have always been amazed at what can happen when we simply plant the good seed of God's Word in the good soil of broken people. We have an expression in our movement: bad people make good soil—there's a lot of fertilizer in their lives.

Actually, the Bible is not silent about who is likely to be good soil. Look at a number of passages and see how clearly they inform us of those who will be more receptive than others when it comes to the Gospel:

Bad people: "I have not come to call the righteous but sinners to repentance" (Luke 5:32).

Poor people: "Listen my beloved brethren: did not God choose the poor of this world to be rich in faith and heirs of the kingdom which He promised to those who love Him?" (James 2:5).

Young people: "Truly I say to you, unless you are converted and become like children, you shall not enter the kingdom of heaven" (Matt. 18:3).

Those searching for God, perhaps in the occult and in other religions: "Seek, and you shall find" (Matt. 7:7).

Uneducated and powerless people: "But God has chosen the foolish things of the world to shame the wise." "And God has chosen the weak things of the world to shame the things which are strong" (1 Cor. 1:27).

The insignificant, the discriminated against, and the nobod-ies: "And the base things of the world and the despised . . ." "God has chosen, the things that are not, that He might nullify the things that are, that no man should boast before God" (1 Cor. 1:28–29).

By the same token, the Bible also tells us plainly where the bad soil is found. Here are some passages that show us where we are not likely to see as much response to the Gospel:

Intellectuals, people of influence, and those of high social sta-tus: "For consider your calling, brethren, that there were not many wise according to the flesh," "not many mighty," "not many noble" (1 Cor. 1:26).

Good "moral" people: "It is not those who are well who need a physician, but those who are sick. I have not come to call the righteous but sinners to repentance" (Luke 5:31–32).

Wealthy people: "How hard it is for those who are wealthy to enter the kingdom of God. For it is easier for a camel to go through the eye of a needle, than for a rich man to enter the kingdom of God" (Luke 18:24–25).

These passages do not mean that God does not love wealthy or ed-ucated people. They also do not mean that people of this kind can-not find Christ. There are wealthy people who come to Christ in the Bible, such as Joseph of Arimathea and Barnabas. There are also some pretty good and smart people who accepted Christ's call, including Saul of Tarsus (who became the apostle Paul).

John Wesley, the founder of Methodism, was considered a righ-teous man even before he received the strange warm blessing that eventually touched two continents with the Gospel. In church his-tory, you will find wealthy people whom God calls to begin church planting movements as well. Count Zinzendorf (an instrumental leader of the eighteenth-century Moravian mission movement) was born wealthy, as was Bill Borden, the twentieth-century heir of the

Borden Dairy estate who left it all behind and died *on his way to* the mission field. In Borden's Bible were six words: "No reserves. No retreats. No regrets." These men didn't die wealthy, but they did come to faith with wealth and privilege. My friend Bob Buford, who made millions of dollars as a successful businessman, has since given the second half of his life to serving the Lord. He has said more than once, "I want the last check I write to bounce." I don't encourage fraudulent check writing, but I love this man's spirit. He wants to give everything he has to serve the Lord. He, and the others mentioned here, are all great examples of God's message implanted in good soil.

It is not that smart, moral, and wealthy people do not come to Christ and bear fruit; the point is that "not many" will respond from these sectors. God loves all people, but there will be fewer who respond in these domains of culture than from the ones mentioned earlier. This is just a true fact that statistics and the Scriptures confirm. If you are called to a wealthy, educated segment of the population, God is pleased and will bless your ministry, but you will not see as many come to Christ as those who work with the marginalized and poor segments of the population. You will be hard-pressed to find a church planting movement started among wealthy, educated people. But it is easy to find them among poor, working-class people.

I often see a look of despair in the eyes of church planters whenever I teach on this subject. For the last several decades, the vast majority of church planting efforts have focused on the poor soil of the middle-class suburbs. One can conjecture a multitude of reasons as to why that is: more financial support to be raised, more new housing and displaced Christians looking for a church, or a safe neighborhood where the church planter would like to live. Many church planters find themselves in the middle-class suburbs, and when they hear these passages as to where to find good soil they feel a sense of hopelessness. That is not necessary. Believe it or not, there is sin in the suburbs; it's just harder to find.

Here are some practical ways I teach people that they can use to find good soil in their own community.

First, go for a ride-along with the local sheriff or police. These are servants of the community who are paid to know where good soil is. They know which bar has the most fights, which corner is the hangout for the local kids, where drugs are sold, and which homes have domestic violence.

I suggested this to one church planter in Atlanta, and he followed this simple advice. The officer told him he should go to Crystal Cove, which had become known as "Crystal-Meth Cove." The man and his wife, with a lump in their throats, began to walk through that part of town praying. Soon a door opened, literally and figuratively, and a church was started that now has started other churches in adjoining neighborhoods.

Second, search the paper for bankruptcies or foreclosures. When you spot one, call the person (if a number is available) and tell them your heart was broken thinking about their situation; then offer to pray. You will be amazed at what opens up for us when we initiate prayer.

Third, find out where the local twelve-step recovery groups meet. This suggestion is not for everyone; you must be a recovering addict to really take advantage of this idea. I don't recommend the groups that meet at churches and do not allow smoking. Go to the groups where the smoke is thick and the darkness thicker. These are gatherings of sinners who realize they are enslaved to sin and are powerless to overcome that sin without divine intervention. They are longing to be set free; this is good soil. Wherever there are drugs or alcohol, there will be these recovery groups.

Fourth, be available at a crisis pregnancy center, or even near an abortion clinic, for prayer and as a listening ear. Leave the picket signs at home, and bring Christ's heart of compassion for women who are torn up inside and needing grace and forgiveness. I fear that in zealousness for the cause of life, Christendom has missed the opportunity to change a life that is in need of our message of hope and redemption.

I believe there is good soil everywhere; we just need to open our eyes and look for it. It is clear in Revelation that there will be people from every tribe, every tongue, and every nation with us in heaven (Rev 5:9; 7:9; 13:7; 14:6). There must be good soil to be found in every people group on the planet. I am not suggesting that we abandon any people group or segment of our society. I am merely saying we should learn to look at each people group with a lens to find the good soil within it, with a willingness to shake the bad soil off our feet.

Jesus had an interesting conversation with His disciples in John 4:27–38. He had just opened the spiritual eyes of a Samaritan woman with a bad reputation to understand who He truly was. She went back to her village to tell everyone that she had met the Messiah. The entire village poured out to meet Jesus as He was discussing the harvest of souls with His disciples. He said, "Do you not say, 'There are yet four months, and then comes the harvest'? Behold, I say to you, lift up your eyes and look on the fields, that they are white for harvest." Of course, the Jews of His day would never have imagined that Samaritans would be a good place for the Gospel, but Jesus did. He pointed to the multitude of Samaritans flooding out of the village to find the Messiah, all dressed in traditional white Samaritan garments,[2] and said, "Look, the fields are white for a harvest, if you would only begin to look in places you least expect" (my paraphrase).

Even though many today will be wearing black, they are truly white (or ripe) for a harvest. We must begin to look in places where traditionally the church would never go, for the spread of the Gospel.

One church planter in Spokane, Washington, who had recently been released from prison himself started reaching out to people in a place that is commonly called "Felony Flats." He began to see prostitutes, drug addicts, and eventually drug dealers come to faith. One day, three local drug dealers came to his house and said, "We need to talk to you. Come with us." He felt a peace, so he followed them outside and into a car. They drove to a vacant lot where they told him to get out. Nervously, but in faith, he got out of the car. One of them said to him, "We just needed to tell you that we think you're legit." Whew! "We also want to tell you that your son has been comin' around looking for drugs again. We have all agreed not to sell him any."

His son called his dad a couple of weeks later in tears. He said that every time he went to a drug dealer he was told, "No drugs; you need to call your father." He gave his life back to Christ and was soon baptized by his father. Can you imagine drug dealers actually helping someone give his life to Christ? Several of the church planters who are part of our movement were once drug dealers. A couple of the dealers from Felony Flats came to know Christ, and now a church is meeting in one of the houses where drugs were once sold. People now call that part of town "Fell-on-Knees Flats." Most churches would never consider drug dealers a good choice for sharing the Gospel, much like Samaritans in the eyes of first-century Jews. Too bad; there is a lot of good soil there.

Finding good soil is not difficult once you get over the fear factor. Good soil may even find you.

One day I received a phone call in my office. The voice on the other end of the line had a Latino accent and spoke in tough street language, but I could sense a kind and gentle man on the other end of the phone. His name was Gabriel. A former gang member, he had recently been released from prison where he accepted Christ and was now living in a tough neighborhood of East L.A. Earlier that day, someone in his apartment had been on drugs and was seemingly demon-possessed. Gabriel had somehow been given my card, and since it said "church" on it he decided to call me for advice, even though I was a complete stranger. We talked for a few minutes about what the Bible has to say about drugs and demons.

Then I asked him if he went to church. He told me that since he had gotten out of prison he found there weren't any churches where he felt welcomed. I then asked, "Would you like to start a church?" There was a long pause. Then Gabriel asked, "Can we do that?" I said, "Sure. Just invite everyone in your complex to your apartment next Wednesday, and I'll bring Michael and Jake along, and we'll start a new church." He agreed. That next Wednesday, a new church was started in the barrio of East L.A. Gabriel's wife, Carlota, was not a believer and was less than enthusiastic about having a church in their apartment, so for a few months we actually met in the parking lot.

Most of the new believers were barely literate, so I bought them the Bible on CD. They would gather in Gabriel's apartment around a boom box, press Play, and listen to the Word of God with rapt attention.

After a couple of people gave their lives to Christ, we decided to have a baptism in the parking lot on a Saturday morning. We brought in a barbecue and let the smell of steak grilling over the fire fill the apartments. Lots of people started coming out for the free lunch.

We started singing songs and filled a little kiddie pool with water. Curiosity kept everyone watching; in fact, the balconies were filled with onlookers. We had the new believers sit down in the little pool, and we baptized them in front of everyone. Then we presented the message of the Gospel and asked if any others wanted to come down and accept Christ and be baptized. Three more people gave their lives to Christ and were baptized. Our presence was now well known in the whole neighborhood, and we were being watched carefully.

One evening, while we were sitting in a circle discussing the Bible, I noticed a young woman watching us. She was not entering into the circle but observing at a distance with her two small kids, simply listening to the Word of God. As the weeks went on, Juanita eventually worked her way into the meeting. She would sit quietly and listen to the Scriptures.

A few weeks later we read about the suffering of Christ. The scourging and crucifixion were described in detail (this was before the movie *The Passion of the Christ* came out). Juanita was sitting on the edge of her seat, speechless. Then I read about the resurrection, and she couldn't contain herself anymore. When I said, "He rose from the dead," she raised her hand and without hesitation asked, "Do you mean His spirit rose, His ghost?" I said "No, not just His spirit, His body came back to life." I asked, "Do you remember the story of Doubting Thomas?" She shook her head. I realized that this girl, who spent twenty years living in Los Angeles, had never heard the story of the Gospel before. She was amazed by the message. I wish that most Christians would have that sense of awe with the story.

After the meeting I spoke with her. I asked her about her kids. They had different fathers, both in prison. I was shocked to find that her younger child never received a name. They just called him Pudgy. His father was in jail, without possibility of parole, a dangerous member of the Mexican Mafia. When I talked with the kids, I noticed that they were shy about speaking. Later I found out from others that they both had serious speech impediments.

The following week, she came to the meeting in the parking lot and afterward announced to me, "The devil doesn't want me to become a Christian because he will lose a recruiter." I affirmed that the devil does not want her to become a Christian, and then I asked her what she did to recruit people to the devil. She said, "I'm a drug dealer. I have been doing this since I was thirteen years old."

I told her she was right about the devil, and I asked, "Do you want to let that cruel and wicked enemy win?" She said no. I asked her if she wanted me to pray for her. She was slow in her response, but determined: "Yes." She turned her back to me and let me place my hand on her shoulder and pray for her. She had learned long ago not to let people see her cry because such weakness can be exploited. I prayed that the devil wouldn't win and that she would become a Christian soon. I didn't feel it was the right time to push her.

The next week, I was upstairs at the apartment complex speaking with someone when I heard a child's voice crying out in joy, "Michael! Michael!" I turned around and saw two boys running up to my fellow church planter. It was Pudgy and his brother. Their speech problem apparently was cleared up entirely. Then I saw Juanita, and she ran over to me and gave me a big hug and announced to me, and to everyone within a mile, that she had given her life to Christ. She told me that she also had found a real job. She had to drive a lot, work long hours, and not get much money for doing it, but it was legitimate, and she felt good about it.

A few weeks later, I was at the top of the stairs in the apartment complex where we were doing ministry. I was talking with a big Hispanic guy named Carlos. He was obviously drunk and still carrying a bottle in a bag, from which he would guzzle every now and then.

He had just been released from custody in the psychiatric hospital, where he was kept not because he was crazy but because he was so violent that they needed to hold him in a padded cell for his own protection as well as everyone else's.

I listened to his slurred story. He was a member of a notorious gang in the area, a designated hit man who had killed some people. He had already spent twenty-one of his forty-three years behind bars. His daughter was now eighteen and living a sordid life, which seemed to bring on a lot of regret but also agitated him. He started to get violent and began poking me in my chest. He said, "I am beyond God's reach! And I don't care! I could pick you up right now and throw you off this balcony and kill you right now and I wouldn't care!"

My brothers, who were with me, were naturally concerned at this point. I myself was calm, cool, and collected—on the outside. On the inside, I was calculating how to get out of his way real fast. I kept looking him right in the eye and said, "You are not beyond God's reach. He does care about you." My friend Joseph, in desperation, got out his Bible and started reading it. Instantly, Carlos calmed down. The Word of God is a powerful weapon; it can calm wild animals and tame vicious killers. I am proud of Joseph's quick thinking. (I was also comforted knowing that before becoming a Christian Joseph was a black belt in Brazilian jujitsu.)

At one point, Carlos even grabbed the Bible, found a favorite passage, and started reading from it. What an amazing turnaround!

I then asked Carlos if I could pray for him. He sighed deeply and said in a calm and relieved way, "Yeah, man." I put my hand on his shoulder and prayed, "Lord God Almighty, I pray that you miraculously sober my friend Carlos right now so that he can hear and remember this prayer." From there I prayed that God would show him personally and in a very real way that he was not beyond God's reach. I asked the Father to show Carlos that He loved him and cared about him. I asked God to forgive Carlos for his life. After that Carlos was slow and tired as he staggered off into the night. I had never seen him there before and, frankly, didn't expect to see him again.

The next week I came to church. By this time, Gabriel's wife was opening up her home to our little church. When I walked into the living room, there was Carlos! He was all dressed up because he was coming to church. He was also sober, very calm, quiet, and even a little shy. He listened to everything we shared. Gabriel and he used to be in the same gang and were both known as crazy guys who would take on anyone. Carlos was particularly well known in the city as one of the most dangerous killers around. You wouldn't have known it if you saw how shy and humble he was in church that night. After the meeting was over he came right up to me and with great enthusiasm said, "Hey, I've been clean all week, man!" Then he grabbed my arm (gently this time) and said, "Listen, come with me—I want to show you something." I was glad to join him but made sure that my friend Jake joined me.

Carlos took us a block away and pointed at a large house on the corner. He then announced proudly, "That's my mom's house. We could fit a lot of people in there!"

We went over and Carlos introduced us to his mother, who is usually very apprehensive about meeting any of Carlos's friends. When she found out that we were Christians, she was a little more at ease but still skeptical. We asked if we could pray for her and her home. We joined hands in a circle in her living room and asked God to bless her home and all who entered it. We also prayed for both Carlos and his mother. When she saw that we wanted nothing from her and wished only to bless her and her family, she opened up to us and made her home available to the Kingdom.

Within a couple of weeks, we had many people meeting in Carlos's living room, and his mother made delicious food for all.

Which would you rather eat: mud pies or fresh fruit pies? The difference is in planting the good seed in good soil. How you start makes all the difference in how you finish.

You reap what you sow, and you eat what you reap.

6

AN ENCHANTED KINGDOM WITH MAGIC SEEDS, FAST-GROWING TREES, AND A BEAUTIFUL BRIDE TO RESCUE

The true well-being of the church: when she
cannot count on anything anymore but God's
promises.

—*Johannes Hoekendijk*

Don't judge each day by the harvest you reap, but
by the seeds you plant.

—*Robert Louis Stevenson*

In the early 1990s, my family lived in a community where there was
a lot of new building going on. In the mornings I used to take my
daughter to preschool. On the way there, we passed some people
putting in a new minimall and a housing tract. There were always
large, brightly painted machines at work, so my daughter was very
interested in what was going on. One morning the workers had a
large machine digging deep holes to plant trees. Heather asked me
what those machines were doing, and I told her that they were
going to plant trees there. I could see the curiosity in her face.

The next day we went by, and twenty-foot-tall palm trees were
swaying in the morning breeze where the holes had been the day
before. With all the creative imagination of a five-year-old, my
daughter shouted out in amazement, "Boy, those trees grow fast!"

I didn't want to tell her that they were grown somewhere else
and transplanted there. I wanted her to believe in magic seeds that
could grow overnight into the clouds where giants live and princesses

need rescuing. There is something beautiful about that kind of faith; we all lose the expectation so quickly.

Oh, to see the world through the faith and wonder of a child! If we want to recapture the beauty of the Church, we need to see her again with eyes that believe the impossible. Jesus presents the Kingdom as something that grows in wonderful and miraculous ways.

In Mark 4:26–29, Jesus goes on to give us a second parable to explain to us the organic nature of His Kingdom. This one I like to call "the parable of how it all grows." It's one of my favorite explanations of the Kingdom because in many ways it releases me from a lot of hard work.

The Parable of How It All Grows

In the children's book *Frog and Toad Together*, "The Garden" tells the story of Toad's adventure of planting seeds to grow a garden. Things begin when Toad appreciates his friend Frog's fine garden. "Well, yes," replies Frog, "but it was hard work." "I wish I had a garden," responds Toad. So Frog gives Toad a package of seeds and tells him that if he plants the seeds soon he too can grow a beautiful garden. Toad asks, "How soon?" "Quite soon" is the reply.

Toad plants the seeds and then tells them to start growing, while he stands there waiting for them to appear. When he sees no response, he tells the seeds to start growing, a little louder. Then he shouts at the seeds, commanding them to start growing. Hearing the loud noise, Frog looks over the fence and asks what all the commotion is about. Toad replies, "My seeds won't grow."

Frog says, "You're shouting too much. These poor seeds are afraid to grow!"

Toad remarks, "My seeds are afraid to grow?"

"Leave them alone for a few days," answers Frog. "Let the sun shine on them. Let the rain fall on them. Soon your seeds will start to grow."

Later that night, Toad looks out over his garden and sees that nothing has changed. "Drat, my seeds haven't started to grow. They must be afraid of the dark. I will read the seeds a story, and then they won't be afraid."

Over the next couple of days, we see Toad reading the seeds stories, singing songs to them, dancing in the rain for them, and playing tunes for them on the violin, all in fruitless efforts to coax the seeds to grow on *his* timetable. One night, in a fit of exhaustion, Toad remarks, "Oh, what shall I do? These seeds must be the most frightened seeds in the whole world." He collapses in sleep from the fatigue of trying to entertain the seeds nonstop for several days.

He is awakened the next day by a jubilant Frog saying, "Toad, Toad, wake up! Look at your garden."

"Oh, at last my seeds have stopped being afraid to grow."

"And now," replies Frog, "you'll have a nice garden, too."

"Yes, but you were right, Frog," remarks Toad, wiping the sweat from his brow. "It was very hard work."

Many of us are like Toad. We are spending our lives singing, dancing, and telling stories to dirt, trying to make the seeds grow. In the end, we conclude that making seeds grow is hard work.

But is it?

In Mark 4:26–29, Jesus tells us: "The kingdom of God is like a man who casts seed upon the soil; and he goes to bed at night and gets up by day, and the seed sprouts and grows—how, he does not know. The soil produces crops by itself; first the blade, then the head, then the mature grain in the head. But when the crop permits, he immediately puts in the sickle, because the harvest has come."

Jesus described the work as casting out seed, going to bed at night, and rising in the day. The soil produces the growth "all by itself." The word translated "all by itself" is *automate*. It is, obviously, the root word from which we get our word *automatic*. The man who sows the seed doesn't even know how it happens.

As I read this parable, I recognize two things that need to be addressed. First, we are all qualified to do the work, and the work is not really so hard. Second, we frequently expend our energy and resources in the wrong phase of ministry life.

In this parable, the man who sows the seed goes to sleep at night, wakes up in the day, and does not know how the work grows. I feel qualified for that role: *clueless and sleeping on the job*. Too many of us experts think we know all about how the work of our ministry is supposed to grow. The consequence is that the mysterious and miraculous element of the Kingdom is replaced with strategic plans, demographic studies, and brightly colored flow charts. We sacrifice pure, organic power for hard work and little results. Professing to be wise, we have become fools.

We also make the mistake of investing great resources in the *wrong phase* of Kingdom life. Innumerable churches in the West spend most of their effort and money on the growing phase of life. Little is spent on breaking up soil, planting seeds, or harvesting crops. Simply browsing a local Christian bookstore demonstrates this fact. Rows of shelves are dedicated to materials on growing—children, families, churches, and schools.

There are very few resources in the Kingdom invested in sowing seeds. There are virtually no resources that are all about harvesting. Because we are not seeing any harvest, there isn't any demand for such resources—not that we don't want it. There probably is a legitimate need for resources in this area. However, until we actually face a harvest, we will not know what works and what doesn't. As Jesus said, "when the crop permits" we reap a harvest. We cannot have a harvest unless the crop allows it. You can have the combines ready, the silos prepared, and the trucks ready to roll, but if the crop is not ripe there will not be any harvest.

Many of our Christian leaders are like Toad. We can jump and shout, sing songs, and read stories, but it will not cause any greater growth. The Bible tells us throughout that only God can cause growth. Trying to cause growth is not possible for us and only confuses people. Worse than that, when we try to cause growth we take upon our shoulders God's work, which can be blasphemous, human-centered, and prideful. This also sets many people up for disappointment when we promise them growth and we do not deliver.

Paul said, "I planted, Apollos watered, but God caused the growth. So neither he who plants nor he who waters is anything, but only God who makes things grow" (1 Cor. 3:6, 7).

It may be obvious by now, but if you skip the important step of planting seeds and spend all your time expecting things to grow you will have few results to show in the end. Pouring more money and time into growing strategies does not create any more growth.

I am confident that if churches invested more time, energy, and money in planting seeds, they would not have to work hard at growing, and the harvest would be much more abundant.

All of us who are invested in the Kingdom of God long deeply to be a part of a spontaneously growing and multiplying movement where God is doing the work. We read the book of Acts, and our spirits scream to be a part of something like that. When we hear reports of the Kingdom expanding and lives changing overseas in China or India, our souls are touched in a deep place that we seldom feel, and it reminds us that our own experience is so empty. It is unfortunate that we sacrifice our heart's desire for lesser things. The reality is that as long as we invest in human-driven efforts, we will never see what we all really want to see.

This important parable speaks to our heart's desire. Jesus tells us that the Kingdom is to grow spontaneously ("all by itself"). Experientially, we are far from this truth. I have been to church services where everything is scripted to the last second. How can we ever hope to see a spontaneous church multiplication movement if we don't have any space for spontaneity?

There is a risk involved in seeking a spontaneous movement. We must trust God to do His part. We must be willing to place ourselves in a position where, if He does not show up, we will be seen as complete fools. Most have not been willing to take that risk. We are often afraid that God's reputation will be tarnished. This fear is not from heaven but hell. We will never see the dramatic power of God if we are too afraid to be placed in a position that requires His deliverance. We will never witness the sea part if we don't take the road that dead-ends at the beach while the enemy's forces are breathing down our necks. In a sense, this is a simple explanation as to why there is so little real evidence of the miraculous in our world. Because we are not in dangerous places, there is no reason for Almighty God to show up and deliver us. There is no reason for God to step in and deliver us from arguments about the color of carpet in our safe sanctuary behind stained glass windows.

Many times I am asked what it is that I *do* in ministry. Bob Buford (businessman, author, and founder of Leadership Network) is also a man pursuing the Lord's call in his life and is willing to lay everything on the line for Him. He recently asked me a great question: "What is it that you intentionally do *not* do that fuels your success?" We should all ask ourselves this question. Our team has thrown out more quality resources than anyone can imagine because of the things we do *not* want to do. Binders of programs and curricula that we have developed stay shelved collecting dust because they fostered dependency upon professional leaders.

To keep church simple and able to reproduce, we have resisted all sorts of dependency upon money, programs, and paid professionals. I once declined a large grant for Awakening Chapel, saying, "No, that money would only ruin what we have. We wouldn't know what to do with it. We would find something to do with the money and soon our ministry would cost too much to reproduce." Fortunately we were able to find other avenues in our movement for the investment without compromising our spontaneous growth and multiplication. We refuse to control the work. We cannot have a spontaneous multiplication movement, such as this parable portrays, by controlling it. We must be willing to release control.

Ralph Moore understands this. He started the Hope Chapel movement, which has grown to well over two hundred churches. He sums up the key to the movement he leads in his own autobiographical work, which he calls *Let Go of the Ring*. The title is a reference to Frodo Baggins, in the *Lord of the Rings* trilogy, who had to let go of the ring of power and drop it into the flames of Mt. Doom in Mordor in order to be free.

We need to be willing to let go of the ring of power and control if we want to be free and see God work. Greater power is found walking in faith and freedom, not in control. Human control and spontaneous reproduction are not compatible.

I often ask church leaders, "Who was in control in the book of Acts?" It wasn't Peter. He had no desire to bring the Gospel to Gentiles, but the Spirit of the Lord did (Acts 10–11). It was not Paul who was in control. He wanted to go to Asia, and the Spirit said no. Then Paul started heading out to Bithynia, and again the Spirit said no (Acts 16). It was the Holy Spirit that was in control in Acts. We have misnamed the book by calling it the Acts of the Apostles. The Holy Spirit is referred to at least fifty-seven times in twenty-eight chapters. If we want to experience the book of Acts today, we must yield control to the Holy Spirit. I believe that if we unite the Spirit of God with the Word of God in our hearts, we will see a spontaneous movement that will astonish the world.

In his classic works *Missionary Methods: St Paul's or Ours?* and *Spontaneous Expansion of the Church and the Causes That Hinder It*, Roland Allen sets a high bar for a spontaneous multiplication movement. We should not be content with less. A true spontaneous multiplication movement is unstoppable. In the latter book, Allen writes: "By spontaneous expansion I mean something which we cannot control. . . . The great things of God are beyond our control. Therein lies a vast hope. Spontaneous expansion could fill the continents with the knowledge of Christ: our control cannot reach as far as that. We constantly bewail our limitations: open doors unentered; doors closed to us as foreign missionaries; fields white to the harvest, which we cannot reap. Spontaneous expansion could enter open doors, force closed ones, and reap those white fields. Our control cannot: it can only appeal pitifully for more men to maintain control."[1]

Spontaneous expansion is true power. This is what we all want deep in our hearts. This is also what our Lord wants. Let's have the faith in the Lord of the harvest and in the seed of His word rather than in our methods and strategies.

Let us find a way to believe once again, like a child, in magic seeds and miraculous trees.

7

WE ALL BEGAN AS ZYGOTES

When the solution is simple, God is answering.
—*Albert Einstein*

The spontaneous expansion of the church reduced
to its elements is a very simple thing.
—*Roland Allen*

American Christianity is dying. Our future is in serious jeopardy. We are deathly ill and don't even know it. Our illness has so saturated our institutions that we are not healthy enough to live beyond the present generation. Our only hope is to try to keep current organizations alive for as long as possible, by any means possible. This is the mentality in Christian "churchianity." Many institutions are holding on to life support, fearing that death is the end of us. Do you think I am overstating our condition? Then it is even more evidence of how bad off we are. Look at the facts.

The Southern Baptists have said that only 4 percent of the churches in America will plant a daughter church. That means that 96 percent of the conventional churches in America will never give birth.[1] On the basis of experience, I believe this statistic is true. Even worse, I suspect that a majority of the 4 percent that do give birth will do so with an "unwanted pregnancy," which we call a church split.

Many people think this state of affairs is fine. I have heard people say, "We have plenty of churches. There are churches all over the place that sit empty, so why start new ones? We don't need more churches, but better ones." Can you imagine making such a statement about people? "We have plenty of people. We don't need more people, just better ones. Why have more babies?" This short-range thinking is only interested in the here and now and does not think there are long-term consequences for living selfish lives. Realize that no matter how inflated you think the world population is, we are only one generation away from extinction if we do not have babies. This is an undeniable fact.

In response to a large population, China instituted a law that each family can only have one child. The Chinese people responded by desiring sons to carry on the family name, and so untold thousands of daughters were killed off by abortion and infanticide. China has a crisis coming that will probably affect us all. It is scary to imagine a nation where men outnumber women by up to 30 percent.[2] Now imagine an army of millions of men, without enough women, governed by a dominating dictatorial group that once viewed expansion of its ideology as sacred. Too much testosterone armed with modern weapons and an ideological cause is a scary thing. When I consider these things, I fear for the nations that are near China's borders. I fear for us all. Short-range thinking in China or in the church is stupid, and the consequences are perilous.

Imagine the headlines if it were suddenly discovered that 96 percent of the women in America were no longer fertile and could not have babies. We would instantly know two things. First, this is not natural, so there is something wrong with their health. Second, we would also know that the future is in serious jeopardy. This is the state of the church in America right now. It is that serious, and we need to take heed.

We need a new form of church that can be fruitful and multiply. Many of our churches do not even *want* to multiply. For many in Christian leadership, *church planting* is a scary term. It connotes pain, hardship, and loss. The separation of relationships, the cost in resources, and the expense of starting churches like their own is too intimidating. This sort of thinking has kept the local church in bondage and fear.

The way church multiplication has been taught scares people. It is often taught that when a group gets past fifteen in size, it is essential that it divide into two groups. No wonder reproduction is not attractive to church members. This feels more like a divorce than reproduction. Imagine if, in order to reproduce, humans had to cut off a limb, plant it in soil, and hope that it sprouted into another body. Ouch! I suspect that if God had designed our reproduction in this manner, we would all choose extinction.

Actually, reproduction is not hard. It is natural. Dare I say, it is even pleasurable. In conferences I often ask people to raise their hand if they have children. I then wink and say, "See, you all already know how to reproduce!" Inbred in all living things is a desire to reproduce. It drives us. Today, you will be faced with advertising and images that appeal to your own sexuality, which is what causes reproduction. Sex is everywhere, because it is so important to us (granted, a little too important to us).

The fact that reproduction is thought to be so hard and painful for churches is evidence of how far removed we are from being healthy and natural. We don't have to buy books or attend seminars to learn how to reproduce humans. In high school we do have classes that teach sex education, but not so much to teach kids *how* to have babies as how *not* to. Reproduction comes from a natural desire inherent in all healthy living things. Do you think Adam and Eve knew what to do, or did God have to give them a seminar first?

Reproduction is the product of intimacy, and we are created to enjoy intimacy. Even among churches, reproduction is the product of intimacy—with Christ, His mission, His spiritual family, and the lost world.

"Church Shopping"

What makes a good church? Have you ever been "church shopping"? What do you look for? I have asked that question all across the country, and the answers are usually the same: good music, good preaching, good programs for my kids, friendly and welcoming people, beliefs that I share, and so on.

The mentality in modern churchianity is often that the bigger the church, the better it must be. More *disciples* and more *dollars* are the standard of what is blessed by God in churchianity.

In his breakthrough book *Natural Church Development*, Christian Schwarz conducted a global survey of the worldwide church and discovered seven important characteristics of a healthy church. One intriguing thing he also discovered is that smaller churches are actually healthier than the huge megachurches. He says, "The evangelistic effectiveness of mini-churches is statistically 1,600 percent greater than that of the megachurches!" In their research, his team calculated 170 variables and determined which factors were the most negative in relation to health and growth. They found that large size was the third most negative factor, on par with "liberation theology" and "traditionalism." [3] How sad it is that the pastors of churches considered small by so many feel inferior to the megachurch superstars. Someone once said, "God must like churches of seventy to a hundred people because He made so many of them." Perhaps there is a little truth to the comment. Those who lead small, healthy churches need not feel inferior. We are now entering the day of the small, and the smaller we go, the bigger our impact on the world can be.

I went to a seminar on how to start a church. Church planting was reduced to simply getting more people in the seats on Sunday. Personally, I want to give my life to something a little bigger than that. In the seminar, the secret to growing a church was explained as revolving around two very important things: clean bathrooms and plenty of parking spaces. Apparently, the Kingdom of God is held up by dirty toilets and poor parking. Jesus will have to wait for us to clean up our act. In India and rural China, however, where the church is growing fastest, among the most noticeable missing ingredients are clean toilets and parking spaces, so I guess the theory espoused is not necessarily true.

My coworker and friend Brad Fieldhouse found an advertisement in a Christian publication that claimed having a new digital sign on the front lawn was the secret to 100 percent of a church's growth. Oh, how far we have wandered from the simplicity and purity of devotion to Christ. Do we really think that our great programs will impress the non-Christians in our community to such an extent that they will say, "Hey, that's a nice sign. And check out the parking lot. Wow, I want to be a Christian too!"

We cannot compete with Hollywood when it comes to entertainment. The best preachers cannot out-entertain Jay Leno and David Letterman, with their teams of talented writers. The best worship band cannot put on a better show than the Rolling Stones, No Doubt, or Green Day. Our buildings are not so nice as the ones that corporate America is constructing; in fact, other religions and cults are outdoing us architecturally. Have you seen any Christian movies? Please! We are not able to come up against the world, play its game, and win. It is a foolish strategy—and a needless one.

Suppose for a moment that this strategy actually works. Imagine that hundreds of people come to us because they are impressed by our music, children's programs, clean toilets, and parking spaces. What if suddenly being a Christian is cool and the newest fad is to attend church. What have we done? Are we better off? I don't think so. Now we have churches full of consumers looking for the one that offers the best "service" for them or their family. Wherever the next great show is, that is where the multitudes will flock. Does it sound familiar at all?

What we draw them *with* is what we draw them *to*. If they come expecting to be entertained, we had better entertain them if we want to keep them coming back every week. This mentality creates a vicious circle of endless program upgrades, staff improvements, and building campaigns to feed the consumer monster. The monster is always hungry. Pastors are burned out. Members are marginalized and lost in the programs. The lost community gets a corrupted caricature of the Kingdom of God.

Imagine if we went "family shopping" and started looking for the best family to live with. What would happen if we asked: "Which family has a nicer house? Which offers better school programs to educate us? Which parents make us laugh and feel good about ourselves? Do we like the siblings in the Johnson family or the Roberts family better?" How foolish this sounds; yet it is not very far from the reality today when we talk about church shopping.

The reason shopping for churches seems more sensible than shopping for families is because church has been reduced to a once-a-week event that is aimed entirely at attracting people. Because we position people to be consumers, they respond like consumers. Advertising may work for business, but if we need to advertise to start a family we are really screwed up. Family is not a choice; we are born into it. Church is meant to be a family that we are born into as well.

We must remind ourselves that there is something better than drawing multitudes to our services. Jesus often turned away from the multitudes and was even known to turn the multitudes away with hard words.

More people attending does not mean success. Nicer buildings do not mean your church is any better. The key to a healthy church is not better messages, better music, better methods, and more money. It is time to abandon those ideas and search for how the Kingdom is truly meant to expand.

In his classic book *Power Through Prayer*, E. M. Bounds once wrote, "Men are looking for better methods; God is looking for better men."[4] One of the driving convictions of our movement is summarized in the statement that a church is only as good as her disciples. Healthy disciples make up a healthy church. Reproducing disciples makes a reproducing church.

Life Begins at the Molecular Level

Reproduction of all kinds begins on a molecular level. We each began life as a zygote. A zygote is a cell formed by the union of a male seed and a female egg. Life multiplies from there. Here is a picture of a zygote. This is day two of a human life.

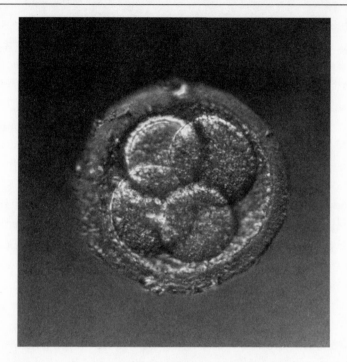

All of us started in the same way. Julia Roberts (the movie star) and Julia Childs (the late popular chef) both looked like this for a moment. The differences could only be discovered deeper, at a more molecular level. We would have to examine the chromosomes of the DNA strands in each zygote to see the very subtle differences. But even then, the vast majority would be exactly the same. Julia Roberts got the good-looking gene and Julia Childs got the good-taste gene (which explains Roberts's marriage to Lyle Lovett, who also once looked like the zygote pictured here).

All reproduction begins at the molecular level and develops from the micro to the macro, from the simple to the complex. It is the same in the Kingdom of God.

The Parable of Starting Small and Growing Large

The third organic parable Jesus presents in the fourth chapter of Mark's Gospel is the parable of the mustard seed (Mark 4:30–32). Jesus said: "How shall we picture the Kingdom of God, or by what parable shall we present it? It is like a mustard seed, which, when sown upon the soil, though it is smaller than all the seeds that are upon the soil, yet when it is sown, grows up and becomes larger than all the garden plants and forms large branches; so that the birds of the air can nest under its shade."

The growth of the Kingdom of God must start at the smallest of levels. Jesus is instructing us that the Kingdom of God must start small and grow via multiplication to have great and expansive influence.

There is much discussion these days about church multiplication. This is my passion and life. But no matter how committed we are, we will never see church multiplication if it is all we speak of. Trying to multiply churches is starting at the wrong place. A church is a complex entity with multiple cells. We must go further down microscopically, to the smallest unit of Kingdom life if we want to start the multiplication process.

If we cannot multiply churches, we will never see a movement. If we cannot multiply leaders we will never multiply churches. If we cannot multiply disciples, we will never multiply leaders. The way to see a true church multiplication movement is to multiply healthy disciples, then leaders, then churches, and finally movements—in that order.

As passionate as I am about church planting, I found it perplexing that the Bible never instructs us to start churches. There is not a single command in all of the Bible to initiate churches. The reason is quite clear: we are not to start churches, but instead to make disciples who make disciples. That is actually the way churches are started, at least in the New Testament. Jesus gave us instruction that is on the molecular level of Kingdom life, for a very good reason: it works. Trying to multiply large, highly complex organisms without multiplying on the micro level is impossible.

Ladies, imagine if you had to give birth to full-grown adults. We should be grateful that we reproduce on a simpler level. But even a newborn infant is complex, and a painful delivery. Life did not begin at birth; it began as a zygote. The moment that conception occurred, all the DNA necessary for the formation, growth, and development of a mature person was intact. The DNA never changes; it just leads the multiplication process within every tiny cell into forming the complete body.

The basic unit of Kingdom life is a follower of Christ in relationship with another follower of Christ. The micro form of church life is a unit of two or three believers in relationship. This is where we must begin to see multiplication occur. Let's face it: if we can't multiply a group of two or three, then we should forget about multiplying a group of fifteen to twenty. By focusing on the simple, we actually can see dramatic results in the complex. A virus is a small microscopic entity, but it can dramatically affect an entire continent in a single generation. At the time of this writing, AIDS is the fourth leading cause of death globally and the first major cause of death in most of Africa today. At the end of 2004, nearly forty million people were infected with the HIV virus; twenty-three million have died of AIDS since 1981.[5] The start of every epidemic is molecular, and the solution for every epidemic will be molecular.

The Basic Unit of Church Life

In a worthy attempt to expand the church via multiplication, many have taken the plunge into *cell churches* or *house churches*. This move toward relational community is a step in the right direction, but to see multiplication we must go even smaller, to the most basic unit of church life. If we can infuse that church unit with the DNA of healthy church life and reproduction, then the influence will spread throughout the entire Kingdom.

The Bible often elevates a group of two or three to significance. Both the Old and New Testaments mention the phrase "two or three." It is interesting that at least ten times "two or three" is suggested as an ideal size at which to conduct ministry. It is not ever "two" or "three" alone but always "two or three." The Bible also does not say "two or more" or "two to five," but "two or three." Perhaps it is good to have flexibility with not too many options. When looking for witnesses in a criminal trial, we are to have two or three witnesses, not more and not less. This is not to be a mob trial, nor is a single witness—one person's word against the other's—enough.

Here are a few reasons I believe two or three is the ideal size for effective fellowship and ministry that will penetrate the rest of the church and ultimately the Kingdom.

First, *community is stronger with two or three* (Eccles. 4:9–12). Solomon writes, "Two are better than one . . . and a strand of three cords is not easily broken" (Eccles. 4:9–12). There is a sense in which a group of two or three is indeed stronger for community than any other size. Why? Not only do they share effort (or as Solomon says, "they have a good return for their labor") but also they can encourage one another well. Solomon writes, "If either of them falls, the one will lift up his companion." It is possible for one to fall in a crowd and not be noticed. But in a group of two or three, everyone is noticed and a single absence cannot be ignored.

It may seem obvious, but it is easier to meet one another's needs when the group size is only two or three. It is also easier to resist the enemy as two or three. As Solomon wrote: "If two lie down together they keep warm, but how can one be warm alone? And if one can overpower him who is alone, two can resist him" (Eccles. 4:9–12). All of us need this kind of community strength as we take on the devil and his cohorts.

Second, *accountability is stronger with two or three* (1 Tim. 5:19). According to Levitical law, no one could bring a case to trial without two or three witnesses. Moses explains why this is important in Deuteronomy (19:15): "on the evidence of two or three witnesses a matter shall be confirmed." Paul carries on the idea of strict accountability when dealing with sin in 1 Timothy 5. He is addressing accusations brought against church leaders as he says, "Do not receive an accusation against an elder except on the basis of two or three witnesses." In other words, our information is held more accountable with two or three people than with only one. This size of a group is better for holding one another more accountable. In a group of five, it is easier for a person to hide and not speak up, but in a group of two or three all are forced to participate.

Third, *confidentiality is stronger with two or three* (Matt. 18:15–17). Jesus instructs us that if a brother sins we should reprove him in private. If he listens to us, we have won him back, but if not we are to take two or three others with us. This is further application of the idea of accountability in a group of two or three. Jesus goes on to say, "If he refuses to listen to them, tell it to the church." It appears that Jesus is showing us the balance between having accountability and maintaining confidentiality. The bridge between these important concepts is made of two or three others. A group of two or three is indeed the best context to blend and balance confidentiality and accountability.

It is far easier to give account of our hidden thoughts and foolish mistakes with two other people than to a larger group. This is especially true if all in the group are sharing equally, and all wrestle with their own honest issues.

Fourth, *flexibility is stronger with two or three* (Matt. 18:20). Jesus went on to say (in the passage previously examined on discipline for an errant brother) these famous words: "For where two or three have gathered together in My name, I am there in their midst." Many believe that these words are the most basic description of church found in the Bible.

Coordinating the calendars for a small group of ten to fifteen busy people is a real challenge. It is far easier to coordinate two or three discrete calendars. The larger the group, the fewer the options for meeting times and places. Finding a place where fifteen people can meet comfortably is certainly easier than for a larger church of a hundred or a thousand people. The options for a group of two or three are vast, almost limitless. A group of two or three can meet at a coffeehouse, in the marketplace, or beside a water cooler in the workplace. I have heard of two or three women meeting at a local park while their small children play together on the jungle gym. I have also heard of two or three men meeting together at the grown-up gym while they lift weights together.

Fifth, *communication is stronger with two or three* (1 Cor. 14:26–33). It is certainly easier to communicate with fewer people. The more voices you add to the equation, the more confusion results and breakdown occurs. Paul counsels the Corinthian church that they should limit the number of people speaking to two or three at a time, with clear interpretation.

Our attention span is not that great. We have technological gadgets that do much of our thinking for us today. I have to look down at my wrist now to know what day of the week or month it is. With a short attention span, it is hard for us to receive more than two or three messages at one time. In a context that was challenged by lack of order, Paul recommended that we limit our intake to two or three messages at a time.

Sixth, *direction is stronger with two or three* (2 Cor. 13:1). Paul wrote at least three letters to the Corinthian church because of its problems; we have two of these letters recorded in the New Testament. He used the Old Testament principle of two or three witnesses to verify the direction he was giving to the church and to affirm the authority by which it came.

In trying to find God's direction, it is useful to wait for two or three witnesses to confirm the direction. This is not a Biblical command, by any means (frankly, God should have to say things only once). But if you are uncertain and torn between a number of paths, the counsel of two or three may help.

Seventh, *leadership is stronger with two or three* (1 Cor. 14:29). Paul suggests that only two or three prophetic voices should provide leadership to a spiritual community at any one time. The others are to pass judgment on the messages. There is wisdom in a plurality of leaders. But too many leaders can also be a problem. If the children of Israel had been led by a committee, they'd still be in Egypt. A team of leaders, two or three working together, is a powerful enterprise, safer than a solo leader yet more powerful than a committee.

In a group of two or three, leaders are accountable to one another, community is stronger among them, and there are four to six ears listening to God's voice.

It seems that God has ordained two or three to be a perfect group size for life. Marriage is between two. God Himself exists in a community of three.

If one can reduce the church to its smallest, most irreducible minimum, it would have to be two or three. If we can instill a healthy DNA here in each group of two or three, the entire church body will have health throughout.

Reproduction is also easier at this level. If you have a group of three and want to multiply groups of two or three, to multiply all you need is to find one other person. By reducing multiplication to this simplest level, reproduction can be part of the genetic fabric of the entire body of Christ.

Multiplication and Death

Reproduction always occurs at the microscopic level—even in your own body, right now. The hand that is holding this book is made up of millions of cells, and each is multiplying. Your entire body is replaced by new cells all the time; that is health. Every few months there is a new you. Imagine what would happen if the cells in your hand decided to stop multiplying. The moment your cells stop multiplying, you have a serious problem on your hands (pardon the pun). Your hand will shrivel up and die.

Multiplication of cells will continue until you die. Without cells multiplying, the body will die. Multiplication stops when death occurs. At the same time, death occurs when multiplication stops. Both statements are true.

It may sound paradoxical, but there is also a spiritual truth that multiplication starts with death. There is a cost involved with multiplication. For salmon, the cost is death. They swim upstream, lay eggs in the sand, and then die.

Grain also dies to reproduce. Jesus said, "Truly, truly, I say to you, unless a grain of wheat falls into the earth and dies, it remains by itself alone; but if it dies, it bears much fruit. He who loves his life loses it; and he who hates his life in this world shall keep it to life eternal" (John 12:24).

As disciples, we must deny ourselves, pick up our cross, and follow Christ. This is all about surrender. This is about confession and repentance. This is about obedience. Where these things exist, there is a dying of self, and growth and generativity will come.

We've got to be willing to give up more than our time, talents, and treasure; we've got to start by giving up our *lives* for the sake of His Kingdom. If we are willing to pay the price—if we are willing to die to follow Christ—then we can see an abundant harvest of souls for the Kingdom of God. The Christians of the first century were willing to give their lives for the expansion of the Kingdom, and they were able to reach the entire known world with the Gospel. Every church throughout history whose members were willing to surrender their lives for the sake of Christ witnessed dramatic and spontaneous growth. This is one reason churches thrive under persecution; the people of God are forced to decide what really matters most. They count the cost and pay the price. They die to themselves, their spiritual lives reproduce, and church growth occurs through multiplication.

I have heard that scientific and statistical probabilities demonstrate that if a single shaft of wheat is left undamaged and allowed to freely reproduce and grow, it multiplies into a crop large enough to feed the entire world population—for an entire year—within only eight years. It takes only one apple seed to grow a tree, yet a single apple tree produces enough seed to plant an entire orchard. Multiplication must start small and seemingly insignificantly, but with time and generational reproduction it reaches a global level of influence.

How long will it take to reach the world through multiplication? If any one Christian alive today were to lead just one person to Christ every year and disciple that person so that he or she would, in turn, do the same the next year, it would take only about thirty-five years to reach the entire world for Christ! Suddenly world transformation seems within our grasp. But it could be even closer than that. If every Christian alive today were to reproduce in the same way, the world would be won to Christ in the next two to four years. What if all of us decided to put everything else aside and focus on truly discipling another for just the next few years in a manner that multiplies? We could finish the Great Commission in just a few years.

Christianity is always just one generation away from extinction. If we fail to reproduce ourselves and pass the torch of life into the hands of the next generation, Christianity will be over with in just one generation. Yet because of the *power* of multiplication, we are also one generation away from worldwide fulfillment of the Great Commission. The choice is ours.

Part Three

FROM THE MICROSCOPE TO THE TELESCOPE

All living things have DNA. It is the chemically based genetic code that dictates life, health, and reproduction. The Body of Christ is no different; it also has DNA. To better understand how a living thing works, it is imperative to understand how its own living cells operate.

Part Three breaks down and maps the genetic makeup of the Body of Christ. The intent is to take a microscope to the Body of Christ and discover where life happens on a molecular level. We then discover how the Kingdom expands from the microscopic to a global telescopic view of a worldwide epidemic movement.

8

MAPPING THE DNA
OF CHRIST'S BODY

Perfection is achieved not when there is nothing
more to add, but when there is nothing left to take
away.

—Antoine de Saint Exupéry

A religious man is a person who holds God and
man in one thought at one time, at all times, who
suffers harm done to others, whose greatest passion
is compassion, whose greatest strength is love and
defiance of despair."

—Abraham Joshua Heschel

The Kingdom of God was always meant to spread spontaneously. It
is viral in its organic approach to infecting and transforming the nations. In several parables, Jesus used reproductive seeds as an anal-
ogy of how the Kingdom is to grow spontaneously. Truth is meant
to be contagious. Proper use of God's Word should be infectious and
result in spontaneous expansion.[1]

According to Jesus, "The kingdom of Heaven is like leaven,
which a woman took and hid in three pecks of flour until it was all
leavened" (Matt. 13:31–33). In the New Testament, the Gospel
spread like a chain reaction, bouncing from one changed life to another until the whole known world was reached. This can and will
happen again in our lifetime if we recapture the intrinsic, and organic, nature of the Kingdom of God.

In his work *Missionary Methods: St. Paul's or Ours?* Roland Allen demonstrates how the Gospel spread through four people groups (Galatia, Macedonia, Achaia, and Asia) under the influence of one man in just ten years.[2] The man was the apostle Paul. In today's experience, a missionary's work would be remarkable if it reached just a single nation in the same time frame. God used Paul to reach *four* such groups. How could he come to a place, leave in a short time, and know that the whole nation was reached with the Word?

Thom Wolf suggests that Paul had a strategy: a universal pattern for following Christ that he would introduce in every place churches were planted (1 Cor. 14:16–17).[3] I call this the New Testament Discipleship Pattern (NTDP).[4]

Studying Paul's methods, Allen captured many principles that are necessary for spontaneous and indigenous expansion of the church. The word *methods*, however, is perhaps a poor choice, as Lesslie Newbigin points out in his foreword to Allen's book. Later the author refers to the pattern as "the way of Christ and His apostles."[5] This demonstrates that Allen's understanding of the pattern extends beyond Paul's works and includes the other disciples. It also reveals that the pattern begins with Christ. Wolf has taken Allen's ideas and gone further in delineating what the pattern looks like. It corresponds to what we consider to be the DNA of the church (discussed later in this chapter).

The NTDP is an established pattern that is easily passed on by both example and teaching. The pattern must meet three criteria to spread epidemically.[6] We use these same criteria to evaluate every ministry resource or method that we deploy, to ensure that it is able to reproduce and spread.

The pattern must be:

1. *Received personally.* It has a profound implication: it must be internalized and must transform the soul of the follower.

2. *Repeated easily.* It has a simple application: it must be able to be passed on after only a brief encounter.

3. *Reproduced strategically.* It has universal communication: it must pass on globally by being translated into a variety of cultural contexts and languages.

In *The Tipping Point*, Malcolm Gladwell says any epidemic type of spread (such as Allen describes) requires a "stickiness factor."[7] In other words, the pattern must stick with people in such a way that it is unforgettable and easily passed on to others.

Allen assumed that the NTDP was an oral tradition passed on to others by Paul.[8] In his earlier letters, Paul referred to it many times but did not actually begin to put it down in writing until he found himself in prison in Rome, where he wrote the letters of Ephesians and Colossians. Then the pattern seems to emerge. A delay in publication of powerful, sticky messages is often the case.

My own experience is that the most reproductive messages should gain impact first by being passed along orally before they are produced in published form. If a message does not spread on its own orally, without management, then it isn't worth writing down. If you find that it *does* spread without help, then you have found something worthy of publication. Producing it at that point helps accelerate the epidemic. We found this was true when we first developed Life Transformation Groups.[9] We actually resisted writing anything down because we found that the simple oral tradition was powerful, and we didn't want to mess with it. Wolf has said in conversation that any substantive truth worth passing on should be reproducible on a napkin while one sits down at a lunch appointment. He calls this "napkin theology." In other words, if you can't pass it on by writing it down on a napkin at a restaurant, then it isn't worth writing down at all.

Christ also passed on simple and reproducible traditions. The ordinances of baptism and communion are simple exercises to proclaim in physical action the truths of the Good News.[10] Perhaps Christ intended every believer to practice these symbolic exercises as a means to proclaim the Gospel to their lost friends, neighbors, and associates. The Church has taken and "sanctified" them to the extent that only the ordained can conduct them, and they are performed only in the sanctity of church halls behind stained-glass windows. We even instruct unbelievers not to participate in the communion (which is a restriction not actually found in the Bible).[11] In like manner, we have taken baptism out of the context for which it was originally intended such that now only ordained ministers can do it in a church building. This takes the powerful practice out of the hands of the normal Christian and away from the public eye where it was meant to be.

Jesus also laid out a simple pattern for prayer to guide His disciples: the Lord's Prayer (Matt. 6:9–13). This is such an ideal tool for passing on potent spiritual truth that today thousands of people can recite it, even many among those who do not attend any church or profess any faith in the One who commanded it.

It is most important to understand that the pattern must be lived out as an example, not just a spoken message. It is better caught than taught. Here are some Biblical descriptions of Paul's pattern:

• It was *incarnational.* Paul lived it as a model for others to follow. He instructed the Philippian church to ". . . join in following my example and observe those who walk according to the *pattern* you have in us" (Phil. 3:17).

• It was *viral.* The pattern could easily be passed on to others. In 2 Timothy 1:13 Paul wrote, "Retain the *standard* of sound words which you have heard from me in faith and love which are in Christ Jesus." He went on to say, "the *things which you heard* from me in the presence of many witnesses, these entrust to faithful men who will teach others also" (1 Tim. 2:2).

• It was *transformational.* Paul was not the only one spreading the contagion. Because of its simplicity and radical life-changing properties, it spread easily. Every new soul transformed became a change agent, a carrier of the virus. In writing to the Roman church, which he had not yet visited, Paul reminded them that "though you were slaves of sin, you became obedient from the heart to that *form of teaching* to which you were committed" (Rom. 6:17).

• It was *universal*. The New Testament Discipleship Pattern can be applied to every culture and with every people group. He exhorted the Corinthians (1 Cor. 4:16–17) to "be imitators of me. For this reason I have sent you Timothy, who is my beloved and faithful child in the Lord, and he will remind you of my *ways* which are in Christ, just as I teach everywhere in every church."

Although Paul mentioned a pattern in other writings, the pattern we've identified has emerged with heavy reliance upon Colossians and Ephesians, plus the epistles of James and 1 Peter. These epistles were meant to be circulated broadly, without a specific congregation in mind. For this reason they are less about addressing specific problems and more about passing on universal principles that apply in all contexts. This is why the pattern is more readily seen in them. The following table demonstrates examples of the pattern emerging in these four epistles.

George Patterson, an experienced missionary and father to current thinking about spontaneous multiplication movements, suggests that what he calls *obedience-oriented education* is necessary to see spontaneous reproduction.[12] Patterson lists seven New Testament commands that all disciples must obey[13] as the starting point of following Christ. One can easily see how these commands fit within the NTDP and church multiplication DNA.

The DNA of Christ's Body

In the organic world, whether crickets or churches, DNA is the internal code that maintains the integrity of each multiplied cell. In every organism, DNA is what encodes each cell with its proper process and place in the body. In the expansion of the Kingdom of God, DNA maintains the strength, vitality, and reproductivity of every cell in Christ's body.

The New Testament Discipleship Pattern

		Colossians	Ephesians	James	1 Peter	
		Churches not planted directly by Paul, nor had he ever visited	Circular letter to Asian churches in the Ephesian area	The internally troubled Jewish-Christian diaspora	Suffering believers scattered throughout Asia Minor	Faith
Divine truth	*Walk worthy* by putting off the old and putting on the new	New creation Christians were to put off certain vices and put on certain virtues (3:5–14)	New creation Christians were to put off certain vices and put on certain virtues (4:17–5:17)	Christians who experienced the new birth were to put off vices and put on virtues (1:18–1:21a)	Christians who experienced the new birth were to put off vices and put on virtues (1:22–2:10)	
Nurturing relationships	*Word and spirit flow* into all our relationships	Letting the Word of God (divine truth) dwell in you affects your attitudes and relationships (3:15–4:1)	Being filled with the Spirit (divine truth) affects your attitudes and relationships (5:18–6:9)	Accepting the Word of God ("the perfect law"—divine truth) affects your attitudes and relationships (James 1:21b–4:6)	Taking in the Word of God (divine truth) affects your attitudes and relationships (2:13ff)	Love
Apostolic mission	*Warfare*	Watch and pray (4:7); stand (4:12)	Stand and resist (6:10–17); watch and pray (6:18)	Resist and stand (4:7; 5:8); pray (5:13–18)	Watch and pray (4:7); stand and resist	
	Witness	Proclaim Christ (4:3–6)	Make known the Gospel (6:19, 20)	Turn a sinner from error (5:19, 20)	Declare the praises of Him (2:9–11)	Hope

From Thom Wolf, *The Universal Disciple: Prague Lectures* (San Francisco: University Institute, 2003).

Just as the DNA is exactly the same in almost every cell of a body, the DNA is the same throughout the Body of Christ, for all its members and in every cell. The DNA is the pattern of Kingdom life, from the smallest unit (the disciple in relationship to Jesus and others) to the largest unit. The pattern is the same and its expression remains constant.

After some research and thinking, Paul Kaak and I have come to understand the DNA of the church to be simplified to three things.[14] They are needed in every part of the church, from its smallest unit to its largest.

- *Divine truth.* Truth comes from God. It is the revelation of God to humankind. It is best seen in the person of Jesus and the Scriptures. In both cases, there is a mysterious connection of the Divine and human. Jesus is both God and human. God authored the Scripture, but at the same time there were more than forty human authors as well. Nevertheless, Jesus and the Scriptures are both without blemish. The indwelling Spirit of God is also Divine Truth. He brings the revelation of God and the frailty of humanity together. All of the Spirit's leading is infallible, though we must note that our own understanding and application of His leading is often full of errors, just as our understanding and application of the Scripture is not always correct.

- *Nurturing relationships.* Humans were never created to be alone. We are social creatures and have an intrinsic need for relationships. Our relational orientation is a reflection of the image of God in us. God Himself is relational and exists in a community— Father, Son, and Holy Spirit. God is love because God is relational.

- *Apostolic mission.* Apostolic means sent as a representative with a message. We are here for a purpose. We have been given a prime directive to fulfill: to make disciples of all the nations. This part of us also comes from who our God is. Jesus is an apostle. He is the Chief Cornerstone of the apostolic foundation. Before He left this planet, He said to His disciples, "As the Father has sent me, so send I you" (John 20:21).

There is an innate and ever-expanding momentum found in the purity of DNA. A life changed by the power of divine truth lays aside the old corrupt things of the flesh and puts on the new ways of Christ (2 Cor. 5:17). This then affects the personal relationships of the Christian as love begins to flow out of a changed heart. Empowered by truth and love, the Christian is unable to contain this energy and follows the Lord's command to take the Gospel to others on apostolic mission in hope of changing this world.

The DNA, however, does not function in a strictly linear fashion. The connection with each of the parts makes a powerful combination. Divine truth is the impetus for apostolic mission (Acts 1:8). Apostolic mission is also fueled by nurturing relationships (John 13:35). Being on mission pulls together unified and loving relationships (Phil. 1:27). But one constant remains: divine truth in the heart is the start of everything. A transformed life, and consequently loving relationships and a life on mission, is the fruit of divine truth flooding the heart of a regenerate soul. It is the heart set free by the powerful atoning work of Jesus that is the starting place for all else. Attempting to start from any other place is not only futile but results in fleshly exercises that yield a life of bondage.

The DNA Pattern Starts with Christ

This DNA pattern of the Body of Christ must find its beginning in the Gospels. If this is truly the DNA of the Body of Christ and is of vital importance, then you know that Jesus would emphasize it. DNA must begin with Christ Himself.

Jesus Embodies the DNA

Jesus is the divine truth. Jesus said, "I am the . . . truth" (John 14:6). He is called the "Word" and God Himself (John 1:1). In the past God spoke through prophets, but in these days He speaks through Jesus (Heb. 1:1–2).

Jesus embodies nurturing relationships. God is love (1 John 4:8). Jesus showed us what love truly is, saying, "Love one another as I have loved you. Greater love has no one than this, that one lay his life down for his friends. You are my friends" (John 15:12–14). John wrote, "We love, because he first loved us" (1 John 4:19).

Jesus models apostolic mission. "For God so loved the world that He sent His only begotten Son" (John 3:16). He was sent from the Father (John 1:14; 1 John 4:9–11) and said, "As the Father has sent me, so send I you" (John 20:21). Jesus is called the Apostle of our confession (Heb. 3:1).

Jesus Teaches Us About the DNA

We also find the DNA in the midst of Jesus' teachings. In one of His most profound and organic messages (John 15), just before His arrest Jesus speaks of the centrality of DNA. He speaks of divine truth when He tells us to "abide in Me and I in you" (John 15:4). He goes on to instruct us in our nurturing relationships when He says, "This is My commandment, that you love one another, just as I have loved you" (John 15:12). He concludes this important message with apostolic mission when He says, "When the Helper comes . . . He will testify about Me, and you will testify also" (John 15:26–27). Love and apostolic witness flow out of living in connection with Christ.

Jesus Commands the DNA

Christ Himself commanded the apostles (and us) to "teach (new disciples) to observe all that He commanded us" (Matt. 28:20). This is perhaps the starting point of the communicable property inherent in the NTDP; this is the contagion. But where do we start? How do we select which commands to pass on and when to teach each one? A few commands are pointed out by Jesus as all-encompassing and summarizing of the entire Old Testament (Matt. 22:40). When one looks at all of Christ's commands and synthesizes them down to a few, it is clear that we are to do and pass on to others these things:

- Divine truth: the great commandment. "Love the Lord your God with all your heart, and with all your soul, and with all your mind" (Matt. 22:37–38).

- Nurturing relationships: the second greatest commandment. "You shall love your neighbor as yourself" (Matt. 22:39–40). We thus show the world that we are His disciples by our love one for another (John 13:35).

- Apostolic mission: the Great Commission. "Go therefore and make disciples of all the nations, baptizing them, . . . teaching them to observe all that I commanded you" (Matt. 28:19–20). "Behold, I send you out as sheep in the midst of wolves" (Matt. 10:16).

In short, the pattern has three applications, which can be succinctly summarized with the admonition toward *faith, love, and hope*. Faith is our response to truth, love is our response to relationships, and hope is our response to mission. This is the pattern of a spiritual life that Paul uses to summarize the Christian life as a whole. It is also another way of emphasizing the DNA:

- *In faith* we are to put off the old person and put on the new person in Christ. In TruthQuest (a guided theological study produced by CMAResources; www.cmaresources.org), we ask how each doctrine reveals old beliefs and behaviors that we must lay aside (repentance) and new beliefs or behaviors that we need to adopt. We respond to divine truth in faith.

- *In love* we are to let the Word of Christ and the Holy Spirit fill us richly (divine truth), overflowing into all our relationships. It flows out into our wives and husbands, children and parents, employees and employers, and into every nurturing relationship.

- *In hope* we watch and pray for Christ's return and stand and resist the true enemy as we do battle with him for the sake of Christ's expanding Kingdom. This is our apostolic mission.

Four times in his epistles, Paul uses *faith, hope,* and *love* in the same sentence (1 Cor. 13:13; Col. 1:5; 1 Thess. 1:3; 5:8). He summarized the spiritual growth of the Thessalonians by saying: "We continually remember before our God and Father your work produced by faith, your labor prompted by love, and your endurance inspired by hope in our Lord Jesus Christ" (1 Thess. 1:3). DNA is what compels spiritual growth in us.

The DNA Is Intrinsic to the Gospel Message

Ultimately, the DNA must find its most primitive existence inherent in the Gospel message itself. The Gospel untainted, unedited, and unrestrained should be the impetus itself for a contagious spread among any and all people groups. To preach anything else is a counterfeit. Unfortunately, too often the Gospel that is passed along is incomplete and thus lacking in transformative power.

To synthesize the message to its simplest form, as a way of scrutinizing other "gospel messages," the apostle John writes, "By this you know the Spirit of God: every spirit that confesses that Jesus Christ has come in the flesh is from God" (1 John 4:2). He repeats this in 2 John 7: "For many deceivers have gone out into the world, those who do not acknowledge Jesus Christ as coming in the flesh. This is the deceiver and the antichrist."

This simple idea—Jesus Christ coming to us in the flesh for our redemption—embodies the entire DNA. Jesus being the Messiah is divine truth. His coming to us demonstrates that He is on an apostolic mission. Being in the flesh, and relational, is the basis for nurturing relationships. This is the seed of God's Kingdom, that our God loves us enough to send His Son on a mission to build a redemptive relationship with us. He did not just come to provide us with an escape from hell; He came to connect with us daily in a transformative relationship. This is the DNA of God's Kingdom.

Dangers of Genetic Engineering

We live in a day of radical advancement of science and technology spiraling out of control. We now have the ability to clone life, and even genetically engineer it. With these advancements comes great responsibility. Medical ethics has taken on a whole new level of significance. When we identify and map the DNA of Christ's body, we also face dangers. Here are some crucial warnings.

- *Do not unravel the DNA.* DNA is only potent when it is together. Once the component parts of the DNA are unraveled, they have little or no significance. It is the same in the church. Most churches will gladly exclaim that they have all three portions of the DNA, but they have unraveled it into separate components and so lost its power. "We have excellent preaching on Sundays, which is where we have the divine truth," one will say. "And we have small groups during the week, which are our nurturing relationships; and a strong missions committee, which is our apostolic mission." The key is not in having a separate ministry committee or program to handle each area. DNA must be whole, intact, and in *every* cell. In other words, every meeting, every ministry, every disciple must have all three components *at the same time*. To break down the DNA into separate components and put them in different places and times is to unravel the DNA. Then life and all that comes with it is lost. Mission without love is dead and can actually undermine the cause of Christ (1 Cor. 13:1–3). Relationships without truth are dysfunctional and toxic. Truth without application in relationships and mission is delusional (James 1:21–25). To separate each part is to destroy the whole thing.
- *Do not subtract from the DNA.* Whole DNA is crucial to the health and function of the body. It is complete in its simplicity and complexity. To subtract even a portion from it has devastating results. Many churches are given to specialization, thinking they will find a unique niche that makes them special. But if we concentrate on one part of DNA and eliminate any other part we will lose the whole of it; death and mutation are the result. Many of the churches in the United States focus on teaching, and if they add anything else it is an attempt to build stronger relationships. One reason churches are not multiplying is the absence of the outreach chromosome. Many churches need a good kick in the A of apostolic

mission. In the human body, to be missing even a single chromosome results in severe retardation, and even death.

- *Do not add to the DNA.* One extra chromosome in the human gene can result in Down's syndrome and mental retardation. A person with Down's syndrome is a person who can love and be loved, but this syndrome is not the expression of the body and life that God intended for us. It is a corrupted form that prevents the person from maturing and functioning in full capacity. I believe our churches are unhealthy precisely in proportion to our mutation of DNA. We have added "stuff" to what God intended, and it has slowed the church and halted all reproduction.

It is quite tempting to add "good" stuff to the DNA. Unfortunately, whatever we add to the three basic components ends up doing two bad things: it dilutes the three, and it elevates the additives to the same stature. It is better to let the DNA remain in its simplicity. All good things can be found within them, so do not dilute the importance of the three or elevate anything else to their level of importance.

Why is DNA so important in a spontaneous church multiplication movement? The next chapter describes the potency of releasing healthy DNA into the Body of Christ.

9

EPIDEMIC EXPANSION STARTS IN THE GENES

Ivan Illich was once asked, "What is the most revolutionary way to change society: Is it violent revolution or is it gradual reform?" He gave a careful answer: "Neither. If you want to change society, then you must tell an alternative story," he concluded.

—*Tim Costello*

You don't get to control any outcome, only every choice you make along the way.

—*Stephen C. Paul*

In chaos theory, random actions often are found to have ordered patterns. *Chaordic* is a new term used to describe "chaotic order" found in the universe and a resulting way of organizing and managing people somewhere in the gap between chaos and order[1]: "'Chaordic' means characterized by the fundamental organizing principles of nature."[2] In the natural world, there is a beautiful sense of design and order. Genetic research is beginning to show us some of the ways in which organic growth and formation are determined. By studying how nature works, new social architects are devising ways to develop organizations.

One of the leading voices in this new science of human endeavor, Dee Hock, is the founder of VISA, the largest business enterprise on earth, with twenty-two thousand member institutions worldwide, 750 million customers, and $1.25 trillion in transactions annually. In *The Birth of the Chaordic Age*, Hock says, "Purpose and principle, clearly understood and articulated, and commonly shared, are the genetic code of any healthy organization. To the degree that you hold purpose and principles in common among you, you can dispense with command and control. People will know how to behave in accordance with them, and they'll do it in thousands of unimaginable, creative ways. The organization will become a vital, living set of beliefs."[3]

This is not just some new business management theory. These ideas are based on a careful study of the created order of God's universe. It also appears that some of these principles were true of the Church as described in Acts.

A question I have been faced with for the last three years makes this chapter of utmost importance. How do you organize a decentralized, rapidly expanding, spontaneous multiplication movement without killing it in the process? Can we be out of control and still have order? I believe the answer is *yes*. We can have order in chaos and structure without control, but they must come in a pattern different from what we are accustomed to and emerge from another foundation. The pattern emerges from the Designer, not human leadership. When God is the engineer, there is an order and a pattern that are healthy, natural, and strong. The church can be chaordic.

DNA Instills Order Amid Chaos

Just as in nature, DNA in the church provides the intrinsic code necessary for control, order, and form. We must have more faith in Christ's DNA—divine truth, nurturing relationships, and apostolic mission—than in our own human structures and controls.

Structures are needed, but they must be simple, reproducible, and internal rather than external. Every living thing is made up of structure and systems. Your body has a nervous system, a circulatory system, and even a skeletal system to add structural support to the whole. The universe and nature itself teach us that order is possible even when there is no control but God Himself.

Exoskeleton vs. Endoskeleton

Compare the two types of skeletal systems in nature: exoskeleton and endoskeleton. The exoskeleton, found in insects as well as crustaceans such as lobsters and crabs, is *outside*—hard, inflexible, established at the start. This structure becomes a limitation for growth and development of the organism. The endoskeleton, however, is *internal*—not immediately visible, more flexible, and growing with the life of the organism. The exoskeleton is the first (and probably last) thing you see with the organism, while the endoskeleton is rarely seen at all, but its support of life is obvious.

The Body of Christ should have an endoskeleton that can grow with the body to meet its needs as it develops. The main purpose of the exoskeleton is protection, while the main reason for the endoskeleton is support and strengthening of the organism. Most churches today, more concerned with protection than expansion, have sought shelter in an exoskeleton structure.

As someone once said, "Our current systems are perfectly designed to produce the results we are now seeing." With the measly results our churches are experiencing, we must revevaluate our current systems. More of the same will only produce the same meaningless results in greater supply. We must see a new system that can emerge naturally and easily from the person of Christ and that will never be a top-down overlording system, but instead one of servanthood and grace.

The structure should not be seen, yet the results of it should be evident throughout the body. Organization must be secondary to life and must exist to help support the organic life of the body. Organization can support emerging life; it can never start it.

In the modern Western world, we have become enamored with models. We seek out new models as though they are the solution to all our difficulties. Even those of us who are advocating organic house churches spend too much time pushing a model rather than the Master Himself—Jesus. I liken models and structure to pipes.

A short time ago, I was doing some organic church training in the state of Washington with my friend and coworker, Paul Kaak. Our host served us dinner, and Paul mentioned that the water she served was delicious. He did not say, "My, what nice pipes you have!" Pipes are important. Without them we couldn't have water delivered to our tap, but *water* is the main thing. We keep the pipes hidden behind floor boards, drywall, and ceiling tiles. They serve a valuable purpose, but it is all about the water.

Church structures and models are like pipes in that they are the means to get to the Living Water, but they are not the main thing. Of course, there are good pipes and better pipes. Rusty pipes can pollute the otherwise fresh water of heaven. Some pipes have a greater capacity and longer lifespan than others, but essentially pipes are pipes, and all pipes serve the same function. Once you taste the pure, clean, and refreshing Water of Life, you'll never thirst again. How sad it is if you give the glory for this to pipes rather than the Spring of eternal life Himself. I am convinced that if the Living Water were to get the attention, rather than the models we use, the world would find itself drawn more to the Kingdom of God.

In organic church thinking, it is imperative that you create structure only when necessary. Life should dictate structure, not the other way around. We often say to church planters, "Do not organize 'it' until you have an 'it' to organize." In other words, do not begin with a structure and an organization. Begin with life and let the structure emerge naturally, driven by the needs and demands of the life.

Occasionally, even organic bodies require some external support—a cast, a cane, or a sling—to help heal an injury. They are not the norm and are only considered temporary until health is restored. If you find that you have external structures holding up your church, look to bring health and internal strength to the church so that the external structure becomes obsolete and you can set it aside.

In a typical institution, one can diagram an organizational chart to explain the chain of command.

This form of structure has a direct line of command from the top down and is rigid and inflexible. It has limited capacity for ex-

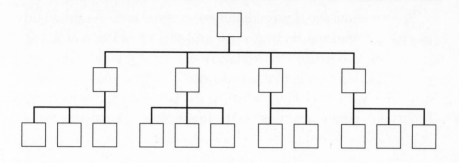

pansion and influence. Worst of all, it is a system full of subordinates, each one lower than the previous level. It is also full of superiors, no matter what disclaimers these superiors offer. In speaking about leaders who rule over others, Jesus said, "It is not to be so among you" (Mark 10:42–44). This structure has a limited scope, both in time and space. It can influence only those who fall under its shadow; it ends when the top crashes, crumbles, or fades away. As Rick Warren said so well, "The shoe must never tell the foot how big it can grow."[4]

In constrast, an organic flow chart (as shown here) appears out of control, scattered, and with no limit to its expansion of influence. Each "member" is of equal stature and potential.

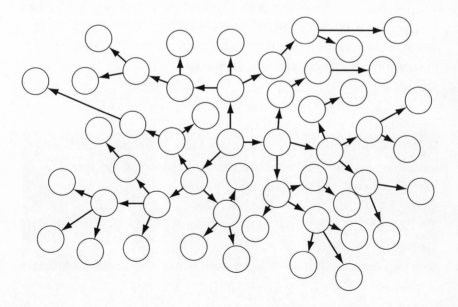

Such a form may suggest that there is no quality control. I find something humorous about this complaint because it assumes that with defined structure we not only have *control* but actually have *quality*. Why do we feel that more control brings about more quality? Actually, much beauty, creativity, and power are lost as we manage life with human controls and restraints. Human controls are so limiting and confining.

Fractal Design: An Organic Structure for an Expanding Movement

In all of nature, there are repeated designs found in the structures of life. These are called "fractals," simple repeating patterns found in much of creation.[5] Each unit has similar patterns and similar purposes. This design can be seen in the most obvious external appearance, all the way down to the microscopic features of the organism.[6] Rock crystals, snowflakes, and leaves all demonstrate such a pattern.

For example, the triangular pattern found in a fern leaf can be seen throughout the plant, from its largest leaf to the closest view. You can see the repeating pattern in the pictures here.

You see fractals in the way a right triangle can be multiplied into larger units. It maintains the same core shape. You can continue to do so into infinite space, and no matter how large it becomes the core shape remains the same.

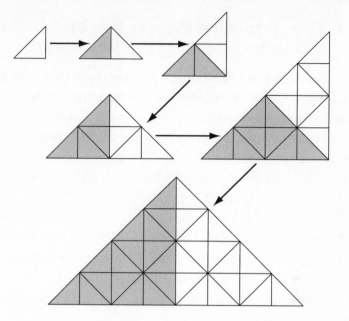

The pattern remains the same no matter how many times it is multiplied. To have a leadership structure that grows with the body, we need to have a similar design that maintains its own integrity no matter how many times it is multiplied. Likewise, a global movement can be divided into smaller units that all maintain the same core formation.

Fractals teach us a lesson for organic church movements. We learn that in nature there is a pattern that holds true at every level of growth and development. This is also true in a spontaneously multiplying movment, where our hands-on control is not possible, or even desired. God's living truth (D), in the context of loving relationships (N) and a global mission (A), provides the integrity in an organic church movement. This DNA makes up the three points of the triangle of our fractal design. It is a pattern that maintains the integrity of the growth and development of Christ's body even in an explosive chain reaction of spontaneous multiplication.

A View Through a Microscope: DNA in the Smallest Parts of the Movement

DNA must be the internal pattern that determines how each part grows. If we use a top-down delegated pattern, we soon find that our form is corrupted and unrecognizable. As each generation follows the one before, soon all are carrying the unhealthy habits from previous generations.

For instance, a photocopy of a previous copy loses some definition in the image. Another generation of photocopying becomes even more corrupted. Every succeeding generation of photocopying passes on the flaws of all the previous generations. Eventually, the image is indistinguishable, and the original meaning is lost. Loose expansion without controls may seem to lack substance and quality, making every succeeding generation worse, but this is true only if we copy each *other*.

The solution to multiple photocopies is to copy from the *master* rather than other copies. So too, we must copy directly from our Master.

In the natural world, scientists have discovered what they call "imprinting." This is described as a chemical process in the brains of birds, especially noticeable in ducks and geese. Upon hatching, the first moving object on which the gosling focuses its eyes becomes imprinted as its mother. God designed this as a way of forming a strong bond between a mother goose and her babies so that they can follow her, be protected and nourished by her, and also trained in "how to be a good goose."

Goslings can imprint on something other than a mother goose. In the movie *Fly Away Home*, a young girl finds a nest of hatchlings, and they imprint her as their mother. At first, this is lovely. She finds loyal companions, and they find she meets their needs. Wherever she walks she is followed by a gaggle of young geese expecting her to feed them, protect them, and train them how to be good geese. This last part is the challenge. As much as she loves them, how can she teach them to fly in formation and to head south for the winter? In the movie, her dad finds a creative way for her to do that, but it is unnatural.

One big problem in the Church today is that believers are imprinting upon *other believers* rather than being imprinted on Jesus. I am convinced that what we do with a new convert in the first twenty-four to forty-eight hours after he or she is born again is of utmost importance. At this very vulnerable stage of life it is important for the new child of God to imprint upon the Maker and Savior.

Usually, when someone is first born again, we say things such as: "You are just a baby. You're vulnerable and weak, and there's so much you don't know yet. There is a mean and wicked enemy who wants to destroy you. You need some good teaching and help, so don't worry about anything but learning right now. Go to church, make friends with Christians, and after you've grown we'll talk about getting baptized and serving. For now, just soak up as much as you can."

We tell these fresh souls that they are helpless, needy, and unable to fend for themselves. We also teach them that their nourishment, protection, and training must come from other Christians, so they never really learn to look to God for such things. The result is that we now have a church full of baby geese, with their mouths wide open every Sunday waiting to be fed. Yet they commonly complain that they do not feel fed on Sundays. They remain helpless consumers, stuck in their nests, who have no idea what it means to take off and soar in formation. They have imprinted upon other people rather than God, and most will spend the rest of their lives soaking up knowledge and doing little with it. Grounded.

In the book *Dedication and Leadership*, Douglas Hyde[7] describes how he used to train good, committed communists. When new converts to communism were found, the leaders wouldn't try to protect them but rather send them out on a street corner to pass out tracts and paraphernalia to support communism, despite the fact that they knew next to nothing. People would question them and even attack their new beliefs, but instead of weakening their resolve it forced them to learn faster and better what they needed to know.

It also resulted in their being even more committed to the cause. It is amazing how persecution solidifies commitment in a follower.

Mormons employ a similar strategy. Perhaps the best reason for sending young people on a yearlong, door-knocking mission is less about making *more* Mormons than it is about making *better* ones. Facing the onslaught of questions, challenges, and debates, these young Mormons solidify their commitment—on the frontline with bullets flying overhead. The internal commitment made in this highly impressionable year sticks with them for the rest of their lives.

I think we are guilty of protecting new believers from depending on God. If we were to follow Christ's example and deploy new believers immediately in ministry, we would see how quickly they are forced to pray, trust in God, listen to the Holy Spirit, and find answers. This would solidify their commitment on a much deeper level. They would have an unbreakable bond to the Head of the body: Jesus Christ. They also would learn to suffer for Christ's sake, which is part of the important pattern that Jesus and Paul set for us (Phil. 1:27–29).

Perhaps this is why baptism was done so quickly in the New Testament. It was a chance for a brand-new believer to make a stand publicly for his or her new Lord, driving a stake in the ground to declare allegiance to the Triune God. I fear that once again we have wandered too far from the plain truth of the Scripture, with dire results. Simple obedience to the plain pattern of the New Testament would serve us well in all areas of church practice. In our movement we baptize as quickly as we can and as publicly as we can. It is not uncommon to have people accept Jesus right there at someone else's baptism and get baptized themselves.

We also want the person who did the evangelizing to do the baptizing. A saying we often repeat is, "The Bible doesn't really command us to be baptized, but to be baptizers!"[8] Here is another example of how conventional church takes the empowerment given to the believer, even the newest believer, and keeps it in the hands of the professionals, thus encouraging dependency upon humans rather than God. There is a reason the Bible comes out and states clearly that Jesus did not actually baptize, but His disciples did it for Him (John 4:1–3).

Paul wrote to the status-conscious Corinthians, who were forming sects according to whichever human leader they were most imprinted on:

> One of you says, "I follow Paul"; another, "I follow Apollos"; another, "I follow Cephas"; still another, "I follow Christ." Is Christ divided? Was Paul crucified for you? Were you baptized into the name of Paul? I am thankful that I did not baptize any of you except Crispus and Gaius, so no one can say that you were baptized into my name. (Yes, I also baptized the household of Stephanas; beyond that, I don't remember if I baptized anyone else.) For Christ did not send me to baptize, but to preach the gospel—not with words of human wisdom, lest the cross of Christ be emptied of its power [1 Cor. 1:12–17].

Baptism is about believers obeying their Lord and connecting disciples to Jesus at the beginning of their new life. It is a way of imprinting newly born followers on their Lord, so that they can look to Him for protection, nourishment, and training. This is the first flying lesson for the newly born-again follower of Christ.

Every disciple we reproduce, every church that is birthed, and every movement that is ignited must be directly connected to the Master Himself in a context of growing relationships and mission. The DNA, in like manner, gets passed on whole and unblemished to each and every generation, thus maintaining the connection needed to the Master. This DNA is quality control for the body, whether we speak of our own bodies or Christ's body. The church's DNA can maintain the integrity of growth without needing human management or controls. In fact, it probably will maintain *better* integrity because it is connecting to the Lord for its strength rather than any human agency.

I feel comfortable releasing control of disciples, leaders, churches, and movements as long as I know that each unit is connected to the Master. This is as it should be. The question we must answer is, Do we trust ourselves with the care of new believers more than we trust God?

Delegated Authority Versus Distributed Authority

Leadership in an organic church multiplication movement never *prescribes* the work but instead *describes* it, allowing great diversity and multitudes of expression, all containing and contained by the original DNA. There is order but not control. There is leadership but not micromanagement. There is accountability of relationship but not subjugation. There is not delegation of authority but distribution of it. Dependence and independence are replaced with a healthy interdependence of the many expanding member communities.

In a top-down hierarchical structure, delegation of authority is important. But there is a vast difference between *delegated* authority and *distributed* authority. All authority comes from God. True authority is recognized and granted from those who follow; however, sometimes that authority is forced by position, power, or even the threat of violent enforcement. This is how the world operates, but the Kingdom of God is not to be that way.

Speaking to His disgruntled disciples, each vying for a better position of authority, Jesus said, "You know that those who are regarded as rulers of the Gentiles lord it over them. Not so with you. Instead, whoever wants to become great among you must be your servant, and whoever wants to be first must be a slave of all. For even the Son of man did not come to be served, but to serve, and to give His life as a ransom for many" (Mark 10:41–45).

Many take Christ's words and apply them backwards. They teach that if you have position in the Kingdom of God it is important to lead as a servant. But Jesus meant us to see that those who first serve are indeed the leaders that others will follow. Position and title are useless in such a scenario. Jesus, of course, is our prime example. He did not have any title or position in this world, yet He spoke with authority unlike any man who ever walked the earth.

For delegation to work, the authority remains with the one who issues the command and is temporarily granted to the one for whom the task is assigned. The authority is secured by being in a position above others. In such a case, the authority above covers the ones beneath in the hierarchy, but it rests with the one above. Each person is connected to the one above in a chain of command. If the connection breaks, the authority is no longer channeled down. If we employ this type of model, we connect our people to others for empowerment and permission rather than connecting them directly to Christ. The mind-set of our people is then to look to other people for all the power and permission in ministry. A codependency is developed that is unhealthy and will not prosper or reproduce.

In a flat structure, one that does not employ a hierarchical leadership model, authority is still delegated, but not from layers above, only from the King Himself. Authority is distributed to each person to accomplish all God has for the person, without needing layers of intermediaries to pass that authority down. One's cover is found in his or her position in Christ, not in human positions above the chain of command.

In this manner, each person is endowed with the authority to accomplish all God intends. Permission from other people above is not necessary if God is the one who issues the command. In such a system, spiritual and relational authority are what is needed in leadership.

Many fear that without positions of authority there will be no leadership. This is a false assumption based on our limited experience of true authority. The strongest authority one can have is spiritual. If the words that come from one's mouth are full of God's wisdom and insight, people notice and follow, regardless of the speaker's position, title, or diploma. This was what was so noticeable in Jesus, especially in contrast to the status-conscious Scribes and Pharisees (Matt. 7:28–29). The strongest and purest leaders do not need to rely upon position or title. Their passion, wisdom, and authentic love carry all the authority that is needed. The moment we rely upon our position or title to accomplish our work, we are sick and dying.

William Wallace (played by Mel Gibson) in the film *Braveheart* had true authority. He did not have any title or position and could have cared less for such things when they were bestowed upon him. What he did have was an inspiring sense of obligation to fight for freedom at any cost. He had the ears and hearts of the people of Scotland. That is real authority. Those who had true position in Scotland did not have the hearts of the people, and therefore they did not have true authority.

In one compelling scene, Wallace is speaking with Robert the Bruce, who is the true heir to the throne of Scotland. With passion Wallace looked into his eyes and said, "If you will only *lead* them, they will follow." Then, with a glimmer of hope, he added extra punch to the thought by saying, "And so would I." For a revealing moment, the prince of Scotland was envious of the authority of a no-name son of a peasant who displayed true authority. He was visibly touched by the notion that this peasant warrior would follow him.

One man had all the position and title, but the other had the authority. Leadership that rests on title is weak. Leadership that rests in a cause and inspires others to follow is strong.

As the banditos in the 1948 classic film *The Treasure of the Sierra Madre* (and parodied in Mel Brooks's *Blazing Saddles*) said: "Badges? We don't need no stinking badges!"

With a top-down exoskeleton structure of church, delegation is critical. Commands are passed down, layer to layer, and are subject to confusion, corruption, and condescension. The church is slow-moving and slow-changing.

Imagine if our physical bodies worked this way. What if the head had to inform the neck, which then passed the information down to the shoulders, which then delegated it to the biceps, then on to the elbow, which delegated it to the forearm and assigned responsibility to the wrist, which passed out the permission to each finger to pick up a glass of water? What if one or two fingers got the message and the others did not? In our body, five fingers can all work in unison in a collective response as a single functioning hand. Why? Because each member is connected to the one head.

A View Through a Telescope: DNA in the Movement as a Whole

Imagine a church movement that is self-organized, self-governing, and self-perpetuating—each peripheral part as well as the whole. Such a movement would foster cooperation and coherence, yet each unit could maintain autonomy at the same time. This is a movement that can adapt and sustain itself despite hostility, diversity, and change. When we first started Awakening Chapels, I envisioned a movement where, if someone ever tried to squash one church, five more would pop up spontaneously. By the time the city officials recognized we were there, it would be too late to do anything about it. We would be immune to city codes, geographic boundaries, and economic restrictions. A truly grassroots, spontaneously multiplying movement is unstoppable—and Satan's greatest fear.

CMA (Church Multiplication Associates, our church planting ministry) evolved in a healthy, Spirit-led way. We found our structure and control giving way to release, distribution, and widespread influence. It is ironic that we had to release control to have greater influence, but this is always the way. Death brings life. Without a crucifixion there is no resurrection. The more of ourselves we gave away, the more we became.

At first, we were just a denominational mission board. After denominational money dried up, we had some people who raised support or grants to fund church plants. We were open to starting churches that were nondenominational and even multidenominational. We evolved into a mission agency of sorts, with support going to multiple church plants, in our own denomination as well as others. As our grants decreased and we did not have money to offer people, a strange thing occurred that we did not expect: leaders of a higher caliber joined us who were not asking for or expecting money. As we followed this development we found ourselves evolving to be something different, but what? An agency? No. An organization? Not really. The best word we could find to describe our movement was that we had become an *epidemic*. An epidemic starts small and virtually unseen, but it spreads from carrier to carrier until it breaks out into a widespread movement that moves quickly. An epidemic can breach geographic and social boundaries. Each "unit," from the simplest part on the periphery to the complex entity of the whole, is a carrier of the Kingdom virus, the DNA of an organic church movement.

We often faced the temptation to organize this growing community. We toyed with written agreements and common procedures, but none ever felt right. We joked of secret handshakes. We felt the Spirit resist these attempts. There was no life in them, so we abandoned them.

Many times we would be asked what CMA is. People would often ask, "How can I be part of CMA?" The answer was always simple, yet unusual. We did not have a contract to sign or a voting process to go through. Applications are not submitted, nor are job descriptions and status reports needed. Instead, we tell people that if they are of the same DNA, they are *already part of the movement*. We welcome them to the family. They become carriers of the virus without need of a central office to check up on them. We are less concerned with organizational affiliation than we are with containing the healthy DNA in each of the movement's smallest parts as well as the whole. Can this work? Yes, I believe it can. My goal is not to build an organization, a denomination, or an agency. My goal is a real movement, an epidemic.

One must ask, What is it that really binds people together into a movement? What holds a denomination together in the first place? My belief is that if it is anything other than common commitment to truth, common familial relationship, and common sense of mission, it is a weak organization that will eventually die a slow and painful death. Such an organization is often dead for years before anyone even realizes it. Many groups are bound by more organizational properties (a contract, financial systems, democratic processes). These things are weak compared to the power of Christ's DNA to hold together a movement.

I once heard of a church, not considered part of my own denomination, that had the same statement of faith, practiced the same distinctives, and was born out of one of our own churches. The church planter was ordained with our denomination, and the core team came from our churches. The mother church was also part of our denomination. It had the same truth, same relationships, and the same mission. But it was not considered part of the denomination. Why? Because it did not apply to be one of the denomination, did not pay the annual dues, and could not vote in the democratic process once a year at the annual business meeting. I am convinced that historians will see this church as a branch of our denomination, no matter what the minutes of a useless meeting held once a year might say.

If common truth, relationship, and mission are secondary to applications, contracts, and payment of dues, then I am sure the movement itself is not strong and will not last. I put more faith in truth, relationship, and mission than I do in the democratic process and annual business meetings convened with Robert's Rules of Order. I am willing to give everything for the DNA, and I do so with confidence that it is enough if we are all attached to Jesus as the Head of the Church. I will leave the control and order to Him. Quality is Christ's concern much more than mine, and frankly He is better at producing it than I am.

So what do you do if you find yourself in a ministry that is hierarchical and held together more by business meetings and contracts than DNA? First, it is important to understand that Jesus loves His bride in any structure or model in which she is found. I often counsel young idealists in our movement, "Don't bash the bride no matter how ugly she looks to you. If you start attacking the bride, sooner or later you're going to have to take on the Groom, and I don't think you want that!"

I recommend that you begin to function with spiritual and relational authority rather than position or title. Defer respect shown to you solely on the basis of title; lead by example and calling, rather than your place in the system. Build bridges of relationship with those who are of like mind and mission. Strengthen the healthy bonds and rely no longer on the weak bonds that are held in place artificially. Let it be that people respond to you out of their love and respect for who you are rather than the position you hold. Make this your ambition more than any title or position. Respect from someone who doesn't know you is meaningless; don't believe in it. Respect from someone who knows you well is the greatest of compliments. We all know people whose position and title are more respected than their person, and that is a tragedy.

The core issue, where all this becomes most difficult, is in giving up control. We are afraid of all hell breaking loose, but our insecurities and resulting control have often kept all heaven from breaking loose. Can we trust the Holy Spirit with our control issues and allow the body of Christ to function in an orderly fashion apart from human hierarchies? It is possible. But is it desirable? I hope so. The world will not wait forever.

Part Four

THE EPIDEMIC KINGDOM AND HOW IT SPREADS

Jesus had a plan. It was at the same time simple yet profound. It would transform a single soul and could eventually transform an entire world. This was an important plan, so Jesus wanted to make sure He passed it on with clarity and precision, and in a memorable fashion.

Like every good teacher, Jesus understood that repetition and practice reinforce an important lesson. Jesus passed on His plan in two sermons. Both sermons are nearly identical. We have all heard a teacher repeat a lesson; sometimes it is because the teacher was busy and did not have time to prepare anything new. But sometimes teachers repeat themselves for emphasis.

In Matthew 10 and Luke 10, Jesus gives the same message on two occasions. In Matthew, He instructed the twelve disciples with His plan for epidemic expansion of the Kingdom. In Luke He repeated the same plan, but this time to the seventy disciples. In both cases, He instructed them and then sent them out to put the message into practice. He wanted to make sure they understood the plan both in principle and in practice. For the Twelve, the lesson was reinforced by hearing it the second time. It is that important.

Somehow the lessons were lost in history. But now, the Spirit has brought back to life the profound implications of Jesus' plan. It is bearing fruit all over the world. This section will delve into the plan Jesus passed on—twice, for emphasis.

10

IT TAKES GUTS TO CARE FOR PEOPLE

Years ago I recognized my kinship with all living
things, and I made up my mind that I was not one
bit better than the meanest on the earth. I said
then and I say now, that while there is a lower class,
I am in it; while there is a criminal element, I am of
it; while there is a soul in prison, I am not free.
— *Eugene V. Debs*

Risk more than others think is safe.
Care more than others think is wise.
Dream more than others think is practical.
Expect more than others think is possible.
— *Cadet maxim, West Point Military Academy*

In a scene from the movie *Schindler's List*, Oskar Schindler glances out a window lost in thought. He is contemplating a move that could cost him his entire fortune. Schindler (played by Liam Neeson) decides to buy his workers from the Nazi concentration camp where they have been taken so that they can continue to work in his factory, but mainly so that they can live. He strikes a deal with Goeth, the head Nazi (played by Ralph Fiennes), to purchase his people. In the negotiations, Schindler says to Goeth, "All you have to do is decide how much a person is worth to you." Goeth immediately interrupts him, with a finger in his chest, repeating the same question with emphasis: "No, no, no. What is a person worth to *you?*" Schindler smiles; he has a deal, a very costly one.

He sets the plan in motion. Suitcases full of money are exchanged, and he begins to tabulate a list of names. His helper, Stern (played by Ben Kingsley), types as the two try to remember each one. This is the story of Schindler's List: one man who spends almost all he has to buy the lives of eleven hundred Jews who are on their way to execution in the camps.

The film depicts the true story of Oskar Schindler, who was not such a noble man. If he had not lived at this time and in this context, he probably would have died unknown. This happened to be a moment when he rose to a task bigger than himself; it marked his life forever and placed him in history. God used a man, even a man as selfish as Schindler, who was willing to open his eyes, see what was before him, and seize the day for a cause bigger than himself.

At the end of the scene, Stern asks Schindler, "What did you say to Goeth to have him give you all these people?" With a look of shock it becomes clear without needing a response from Schindler. "You're not buying them? You're buying them! You're paying him for all these people?"

At the completion of the typing, he lifts the list with a sense of reverence. He holds it up to his friend Oskar with a newfound respect, and he says, "The list is an absolute good. The list is life."

A True Heart of Compassion

We all have people around us who need to be set free by the Good News of Jesus Christ. Friends, family, extended relatives, associates, neighbors . . . there are people around us who need Jesus. In our training we ask people to make a list of everyone they know who needs Jesus.

We so often go through life and do not think about what is going on around us. Not being pressed by Nazis, concentration camps, and gas chambers makes it easy not to sense the urgency of our day. But it is there nonetheless. All around us is the urgency of a moment of crisis, a moment in which we can rise to a task nobler than ourselves—or not.

The Heart of the Epidemic

We all know what it is like to be busy. Jesus also knows. Matthew describes Jesus' things-to-do list this way: "Jesus was going through all the cities and villages, teaching in their synogogues and proclaiming the gospel of the kingdom, and healing every kind of disease and every kind of sickness" (Matt. 9:35).

Jesus was serving an area forty miles wide and seventy miles long, roughly the size of Puerto Rico. The ancient historian Josephus tells us that there were some two hundred cities and villages in this area and that the minimum population of a village there and then was fifteen thousand.[1] This means Jesus was ministering to at least three million people at this time.[2] He was teaching, preaching the Gospel, and healing every kind of disease and sickness. In a population of that size in the first century, He would have been extremely busy. Health care workers today could probably not begin to comprehend the task that Jesus faced.

It is comforting to know that, in the midst of my hectic life and schedule, Jesus can understand and empathize with me. He was busy like I am, but that is where the similarities end. For me, the busier I get, the less I care about others. It is a flaw that I think many of us share. But not so with Jesus. Matthew says, "Seeing the people, He felt compassion for them" (Matt. 9:36). I tend to run past people when I am busy. I get frustrated at slow cars in front of me, long lines, and traffic jams. When Jesus saw the crowds, He saw more than an obstacle getting in the way of His mission. He saw His mission, and He felt compassion for them.

The translation "felt compassion" is a clue to the depth of His caring. There are levels of compassion. Many times, compassion is a second thought for me, rather than an instinctual or gut-level response. After I see someone who is hurting, I have to remind myself that I am a follower of Christ and I should care. This is a shallow form of compassion but, I guess, better than none at all. For Jesus, however, His body reacted to His compassion. It was an immediate and physical response. He felt it. Actually, in the original language this is one word: *splancthna*. The words doesn't sound very pretty, and for good reason. This word for compassion is quite descriptive; it literally means "bowels."

When we want to express love and compassion today, we choose another part of the anatomy, a different organ: the heart. "Heart" sounds so much nicer than "bowels," doesn't it? (It is understandable why Hallmark hasn't capitalized on this ancient expression of love. Imagine writing your loved one a Valentine card that says, "Honey, I love you with all my bowels." Talk about a moving experience—pun shamefully intended!)

There is a good reason for using this descriptive word. When you really feel emotional, where do you feel it? Not in your heart but in your gut. We don't get butterflies in our heart; we get them in our stomach. The first time we men picked up the phone to call a special girl and ask her out, we felt it in our *splancthna*. The first time you women felt the boy's arm go around your shoulders at the movies, you felt tingly in your *splancthna*. When the doctor has crushing news from the results of your blood test or biopsy, you feel it first in your *splancthna*. (If you feel it in your heart, call 911 because that is *not* a good sign.)

So when Jesus saw all the people, his breath was taken away. He was hit in the solar plexus. He was bent over in discomfort.

Most of us are surrounded daily by people who do not have Christ, yet we walk through life without feeling it in our *splancthna*. Why? Because we don't see them the way Jesus does. But we can.

The Bible reveals why He felt compassion for them. It is because He saw them as distressed and downcast, like sheep without a shepherd. The two words translated as *distressed* and *downcast* are also highly descriptive. They are violent words. *Distressed* can be translated as "harassed," or even as "molested." The word *downcast* is a wrestling term that can be translated as "pinned down by force."

If you want to understand the compassion of Christ for lost people, then consider these words in a new context. Imagine you are walking along a park path in the twilight enjoying the evening sky when you hear a muffled noise and some heavy grunts. As you instinctively turn to look, you are overcome by the scene that fills your vision. A big man has violently pinned down a little girl and is molesting her. I am sorry for the awful thought, but it is important for us to get into the heart of Jesus here. He sees lost souls this way, molested and violently pinned down. If you saw this scene, you would not think twice about whether or not you should care. Instinctively and immediately, you would be overcome by rage and disgust. You would be moved to rapid response.

I must confess that I don't usually view lost people this way, and this is why compassion is a second thought for me rather than a blow that knocks the wind out of my lungs. I often see the sin and judge the sinner. Instead of hating the sin and loving the sinner, I find the opposite too often in my life. When I see a gang of thugs spray painting a wall or vandalizing some property, I think to myself that these are wicked people who deserve punishment. When I see an angry mob of Muslims shooting guns in the air and burning an American flag on TV, I feel disgust and wish for justice, not compassion. When I see a drunk man stagger out of a bar in the wee hours of the morning, I think, *What a fool. I hope he gets what he deserves for being so stupid.* The natural response we have is not the spiritual response of one who sees through the eyes of Jesus and feels the *splancthna* of Jesus.

Imagine how different church, and ultimately our world, would be if we all began to look past the calloused exterior of these sinners and saw them as they truly are: molested and violently pinned down by a wicked brute. As we can begin to see past surfaces to the true state of people's souls, we become people of compassion like Jesus. Those who are lost in bondage respond to this kind of compassion—we have seen it happen. As I survey the fast-growing team of church planters in our movement, I see former drug dealers, gang bangers, child molesters, murderers, prostitutes, and pimps. They have all found the *splancthna* of Christ and now walk in freedom and compassion. Terrorists, satanists, addicts, and atheists are now devoted to the One who looked upon them with compassion and said, "I have not come to judge the world but to save it" (John 3:17).

Jesus saw lost people as sheep without a shepherd. Having grown up on the beaches of Los Angeles, I do not have much experiential knowledge of sheep. In fact, everything I know about animals I learned on the Discovery Channel watching the Crocodile Hunter. There have not been too many episodes about sheep on that program. Can you imagine Steve Irwin in his Aussie accent saying, "Crikey, these are the most dangerous sheep in the world! Danger! Danger! Danger!" Not likely.

But one thing I did learn in high school biology is that every species has its own built-in defense mechanisms. God, in His wisdom, placed within all living things the desire to survive and the means to do so.

So I ask, what is the mechanism of self-defense of the common sheep? Is it lightning-quick speed? No, not with those big round bodies and short legs. Is it their ferocious roar and sharp teeth? Nope. Is it the incredible camouflage? Puffy white creatures on rolling green hills? I don't think so. We all know it isn't their quick intelligence and cunning strategic thinking.

Some who are a little more in the know might respond to this question by saying that sheep have strength in numbers. To a wolf pack, however, that is the difference between a single entree and an all-you-can-eat buffet! It is true that after the wolves are full and ready to take a nap, there will still be some sheep left alive for the next time, but that isn't very encouraging to the ones who were eaten today.

When God created sheep, He designed them to live in a symbiotic relationship with another species. They provide wool and food for humans, who in turn provide food and protection for the sheep. He designed them to need a shepherd so that He can teach us how much we need Him. A lone wolf is still a dangerous thing. A lone sheep is wolf chow. It is helpless and hopeless.

How can we possibly expect lost people without Christ to make righteous decisions and live moral lives? That is like expecting a lone sheep to fend off a pack of vicious wolves using its nonexistent strategic cunning and ferocious growl. So I suggest we not expect moral wisdom and righteous actions from lost people. We need to stop judging them and start feeling compassion for them, as Jesus did.

The Converts Are the Workers

The Bible tells us that He looked out and saw the multitudes and felt compassion for them. Then He said, "The harvest is plentiful, but the workforce is too small." He commanded us to beseech the Lord of the harvest to thrust out workers into His harvest fields. At the time, there were only Jesus and His few disciples facing the entire world population. My question is simple: Where did they expect the answer to these prayers to come from? When they heard Jesus tell them to beseech the Lord for more workers, in their mind and context what would be the source of these workers? A host of angels? Of course not. The workers for the harvest must come from the harvest. There can be no other intent in the mind of Jesus or His disciples. Unfortunately, this is not the case for most Christians today.

We have made a terrible mistake by separating the convert from the worker. They are not two, but one. Each new convert is a new worker. We sin when we expect the convert to wait a while, any time at all, to become a worker. Each new convert is a worker—immediately.

This may shed important light on the use of the word *ekballō*, or "casting out" of workers. This is the same word used to describe the "casting out" of demons. It is yet another violent term used in this paragraph. Redemption of souls is a battle against darkness. It is war! Satan will do all he can to prevent this kind of redemption, not just to keep his captive slaves but also to prevent the raising of an army of redeemed warriors.

Perhaps there is one important, sweeping, and dramatic action that takes a person from being held captive to the bondage of sin and demonic deception and frees the person to the mission of bringing the same freedom to others. Salvation is not just eternal fire insurance; it is a new life in the world—*now!* We are set free to be change agents of God's Kingdom. Freely we receive and thus freely we should give (Matt. 10:8). Perhaps God means the casting off of bondage and the casting out of workers to be a single, redemptive move in a person's life.

We are not to wait for a while, as though the new converts are lacking anything. What are they missing? They are sealed in the Holy Spirit. They gain immediate and constant access to Almighty God. They have the power of the Scriptures available. They inherit all that comes with being children of God. They are washed clean of all sins and blights against heaven. Why do we think they need something more from us? What arrogance it is for us to attempt to add *our* training to all that God has already given them. What blasphemy it is for us to tell people they are not ready to be a worker until they have been through *our* curriculum!

The only difference spiritually between a day-old believer and one who has walked with God for decades is maturity. The spiritual empowerment is the same. Maturity does make a big difference, but remember that maturity is gained through experience, not by learning in a vacuum void of hard decisions and pressing temptations. Start the new believer in the process of gaining maturity sooner rather than later. Do not delay the journey to maturity because the person lacks maturity.

For most of us, the rest of our lives are spent learning what it is we already have been given the moment we began the salvation process. How much more quickly we can set new believers on this journey if we also assume they have received all they need to live a godly life in Christ Jesus (2 Pet. 1:3; Eph. 1:3).

The Holy Spirit is a better teacher than we are. The Spirit of God is a better strengthener (or comforter) than we are. The Holy Spirit is a better evangelist and trainer in evangelism than we are. Best of all, the Holy Spirit is a constant presence, which we cannot be.

When we allow, or even demand, that new converts wait and receive instruction and training before they can become workers, we are effectively granting them permission to be passive, inactive, selfish, and stagnant. This is exactly where many of our churches are. We have taught people to be consumers rather than workers. We have separated the workers from the harvest.

I am noticing that a large number of Christians in America feel inadequate about their preparedness to serve God. Why is that? They feel they don't know enough, when they already know much more than young teenage girls in rural China who are starting hundreds of churches. What is really lacking? Knowledge is not lacking; obedience is. Christians in America are already *educated beyond their obedience*, and more education is not the solution.

I'm reminded of the very first "international missionary" sent by God to another nation. We don't even know his name; all we know is his occupation and nationality. He was the Ethiopian eunuch whom God sent Phillip to evangelize in Acts 8. Phillip arrived on the scene, answered the eunuch's questions, led him to Jesus, and baptized him. The next thing we know is that Phillip dematerialized and was beamed to another place. The eunuch went on to Ethiopia with nothing more than some Old Testament Scripture in his hand and the Holy Spirit in his heart. I must ask: Is that enough? He didn't go through the newcomer's class or the new discipleship curriculum. He hadn't read the Bible yet or learned basic hermeneutics (the art of Bible interpretation). Was God being irresponsible? I don't think any of us would claim that He was. Perhaps we need to increase our faith in the Holy Spirit and His word, and what that can mean in a new life. I believe one reason the Lord took Phillip away so dramatically was to establish for all of us that the Lord can use a new convert as a worker immediately. In this story, we are prevented from blaming Phillip for being irresponsible because all responsibility lands on God's shoulders.

New Converts Can Often Be More Effective

Maturity is a beautiful gift that God grants in increments. Even so, new converts often show more effectiveness than those who have been Christians for a long time. Much of this is because the transformed heart is so evident to all who are around the new life. There is also the advantage of still having relationships with friends who are not Christians that makes them more potent agents for the spread of the Kingdom. Additionally, these new workers still speak the language and know the culture of those who are part of their world prior to coming to Christ. All these advantages are lost if we immobilize new converts out of a desire to protect them.

Joe (I'll use a pseudonym) is one of the most intelligent men I have met, but he was also a self-proclaimed Satanist. He reads almost a book a day and can quote ancient Greek poets off the top of his head. We met Joe through our active presence at a local coffee-house called Portfolios.

One evening, we had a visitor at Awakening Chapel who is a missionary and an expert at using apologetics in evangelism. Many had heard of our success with reaching people often neglected by other churches, so visitors were a common thing. This particular man had taught me much and I was excited to have him with us. After experiencing a time of worship in an Awakening Chapel, he commented, "Oh, I see if you lower the lights and use candles and incense you can reach postmoderns." I was a little disappointed in his observations; Awakening is so much more than that. I decided that the best way for him to see the heart of this new church was to take him to Portfolios to see where we do much of our relational evangelism.

At Portfolios, my friend ran into Joe the Satanist. In the course of their conversation, Joe made some comment about what a good man and teacher Jesus was. This started my apologetically trained friend on a logical message based on Jesus' own words declaring to be God. Because Jesus claimed to be God, He is either the Lord, or He is a liar, or He is a lunatic—but He can not logically be just a good man or teacher. This is an argument that the scholar C. S. Lewis first penned.

The talented evangelist launched into this argument but did not get very far. As he explained the first point, Joe then jumped in and finished the rest of the argument. Then he commented that he had read all of Lewis's works and that Lewis was one of his favorite authors. Joe turned and walked away, untouched by the attempts of the evangelist.

About a week later, Joe came to an Awakening meeting. During a break in the service he went outside with some of our newer converts to smoke a cigarette and chat. I noticed Joe was talking with Michelle, the young woman who had just become a Christian in my home a few weeks earlier (mentioned in Chapter Four). Remembering how easily Joe dispatched the veteran evangelist, I was quite concerned for her. I thought to myself that a guy like Joe could really confuse a new believer like Michelle.

Later I pulled her aside to see how she was doing. "I noticed you were talking with Joe. He's a handful. Are you OK?" She replied, "Oh yeah, I'm fine. He just kept talking and talking and I kept listening and listening. Finally at one point he stopped to take a breath and I jumped in and said, 'Joe, you're too smart for me. I can't keep up with you.'" Then she cocked her head to the side just a little, paused, and added, "'But I sense that you're lonely.'" She paused to let that settle in and then added: "'I was lonely too. For many years I would go to bed at night and wonder if anyone in the whole universe cared if I would wake up the next day or not. Then I met Jesus, and I don't go to bed lonely anymore. I know that Jesus loves me and He cares about what is going on in my life.'"

For the first time, Joe was silent. Michelle had struck right to the heart of his soul. This wasn't a peripheral discussion about theoretical facts. This was his life, his need, his core identity that Michelle had intuitively hit upon. This new believer was more adept at communicating what mattered to the heart of a lost friend than was a seasoned veteran missionary.

A short time later, I bumped into Joe and we had an interesting conversation. He casually mentioned to me that he was thinking of changing his religion. I thought to myself that any change was a step in the right direction. Fortunately, I had the wherewithal to refrain from actually saying so.

I asked, "Oh, what are you thinking of changing it to?"

He answered, "I'm either going to become a Christian or a Buddhist."

At that point I had a choice. I could ask him why on earth he would want to be a Buddhist and then he could defend Buddhism for the next hour. Or ask him why on earth he'd want to be a Christian and let him defend Jesus to me. I chose the latter. This time, my instincts proved wise.

Joe said, "The thing that attracts me to Christianity more than any other religion is the concept of *grace*. No other religion has this. The fact that we can receive God's blessings without having to do anything to earn it is amazing to me. And the fact that we can be blessed in spite of all the bad things we do is even more remarkable." Then he went on to describe the cross and how Jesus died even though we are all sinners. Joe's eyes watered up. He preached the gospel to himself that day; if he'd given an altar call I'd have gone forward myself. Joe did not receive Jesus that afternoon, but I believe he is on the way.

My first instinct was to rush to Michelle's aid and protect her from the Satanist. That actually sounds right, doesn't it? Because I was unable to do so, not only is Michelle better off in her faith but Joe is several steps closer to finding Christ.

There are two closely related sins we need to repent of in the Western church. We need to repent of underestimating what God can do through a new believer. Second, we need to repent of overestimating our own value in helping new converts grow and become strong believers. The real sting in these assumptions is that we think we are better able to help people than the Holy Spirit Himself is. We end up creating a sense of dependency on human help rather than on the Holy Spirit—the divine Helper—and this is prevalent in all the church does today.

Let's be careful not to take the place of the Holy Spirit in the formation of new souls. For one thing, to do so is treading on sacred ground where we ought not to tread. Also, we are far inferior to His ability to teach and transform, and the results are quite telling. We have developed an entire generation of dependent consumers waiting for their leaders to spoon-feed them the Bible verse of the week, rather than an army of Kingdom agents ready to transform our culture with the power of the Gospel. The world sees no difference between the Christian and the non-Christian because we are demonstrating little or no difference in how we live our lives. If we actually think that having our good teaching curriculum will make the difference, we are more deceived than we realize.

You might assume that the implication of this thinking is that we leave new babes in Christ alone without any human assistance. That is misinterpreting my words and my intent. We should be a part of "teaching them to observe all that [Jesus] commanded" (Matt. 28:20), but the key term is "to observe." We need to get them involved in obeying immediately.

Nevertheless, we must also realize that Jesus' pattern was to send people out early rather than keep them back in a safe place. He is the one who said, "Behold, I send you out as sheep in the midst of wolves" (Matt. 10:16). He sent the Ethiopian eunuch (Acts 8:26–40), the Gerasene Demoniac (Mark 5:1–20), the Samaritan woman (John 4:1–42), and the man born blind (John 9:1–41) out into the public to do ministry immediately, with little or no human assistance. Perhaps God would greatly honor this type of faith because it is placed in Him more than in us, for all our efforts to be so responsible for people's spiritual growth. Remember that it is God who causes the growth (1 Cor. 3:6–7), not us.

Jesus also challenges us with the example of Matthew the tax collector. In Matthew 9:9, Jesus looks in the tax office and calls out to Matthew. He saw a tax collector, the most notorious of sinners, and said to Himself, *Ah, now there is an apostle!*

Tax collectors were so hated that they had a classification all their own. Jesus' enemies accused him of spending time with the "sinners *and* the tax collectors." It's as though there is a special place in hell reserved solely for these spiritual criminals. Tax collectors are not popular people in any day or culture, but especially not at that time. They were considered to be traitors to their people, not just because they were corrupt but also because they stole money from the Jews to pay the oppressive Roman governors.

The same day he was called, Matthew brought all of his friends and relatives to his house to meet Jesus for a party. When Jesus issued the challenge to pray for workers for the harvest, it was directed to this same Matthew, who was sent as a worker just a couple of verses later (in Matt. 10:1–5). Matthew was not alone, nor was he left without any additional training, but he also didn't passively receive his training. He was an active worker from the very beginning.

I find it ironic and beautiful that of the four Gospel accounts it is Matthew's that was written especially to the Jews. If I were to choose a man to write my Good News for the Jews, I would choose a man of utmost integrity who would have ready credibility among the Jewish leaders. I would probably go to the Temple and find the wisest and most respected young Pharisee I could and choose him to be my Gospel writer. Jesus went to the tax office and chose the most hated and disrespected man He could find. When he wanted to bring the good news to the Gentiles, then he went to the temple and chose a Pharisee (Saul of Tarsus).

I think the reason the Lord of the harvest does things this way is so that the glory and credibility is found in Him and the changed life He has produced, rather than in human wisdom or power (1 Cor. 1:26–31). We should strive to find ways of glorifying the Lord by changed lives rather than by our own efforts and teaching.

The epidemic begins with the right heart for people. If we do not start with seeing the world through the eyes and guts of Jesus, we will not have the heart to even get started. Motivation is crucial.

After Jesus gave us an example of why we should care for lost people, He went on to give us practical principles for how to start an epidemic movement. People are sometimes surprised at how pragmatic Jesus was in His instruction. The next chapter brings these pragmatic principles to light.

There are only a few movies that have touched me as deeply as *Schindler's List*. After the credits passed and the lights turned on, I was still seated in deep thought, wiping away my tears.

It was a scene near the end of the movie that struck me the hardest, a scene in which Schindler realizes, as if for the first time, what a person is truly worth. When I first saw this, I felt as though I'd gotten punched right in the *splancthna*.

The war is over, the Allies have won, and suddenly Schindler finds himself on the run as a registered member of the Nazi party. He walks out to his car with instructions to Stern to care for the eleven hundred workers who are all present and alive.

Before he leaves, the workers present a gift to Schindler. Earlier, wanting somehow to express their appreciation, they decided to pull teeth from workers, melt the gold fillings, and cast a ring. On the ring is an inscription in Hebrew from the Talmud; it says, "He who saves a life saves the world entire."

Schindler is deeply moved when presented with this gift from these people who have nothing but their lives. He reaches out to shake Stern's hand. He cannot contain himself, so he utters in barely a whisper a confession from his heart, "I could have got more out." Stern shakes his head, not accepting this assessment: "Oskar, there are eleven hundred people alive here because of you. You did so much. There will be generations alive because of what you did." Schindler seems to not hear the comforting words and goes on: "If I had only made more money." He starts to laugh and cry at once and states, out loud, "I threw away so much money."

The confession is freeing, yet he goes further. "This car. Why did I keep the car? Goeth would have bought the car. That could have been ten more people, right there." As he starts to stumble on the drive in deep contemplation, he pulls a little gold pin with a swastika on it and remarks, "This pin could have been two more people. It is gold. It would have bought me two more people." He starts doing the math in his head and mumbles to himself, "At least one more, it would have got one more . . . one more person for this pin." He then stumbles back to the car and doubles over in sobs as he realizes, "I could have saved one more person, and I didn't. A person, Stern."

His compassion in this moment came from deep in his bowels. This is *splancthna*.

The scene ends with Oskar and his wife driving away in the car with the reflection of hundreds of saved lives watching. I have seen this scene dozens of times, and yet my eyes still tear up. It is to me perhaps the most powerful scene in all of film.

Only Jesus can save people. He is the one who purchases, or redeems, us from the clutches of the enemy. We are not responsible for others' faith, but we are the agents who bring the message: "We are ambassadors for Christ, as though God were entreating through us; we beg you on behalf of Christ, be reconciled to God" (2 Cor. 5:20). We do not do this under a sense of shame or guilt but are moved by the love of Christ. His compassion lives in us.

No matter how much we do in this life to release the captives that the enemy intended to destroy, we will still look back and realize how much more we could have done. Like Stern, Jesus will say, "You did so much. There will be generations that are alive because of what you have done."

Oskar Schindler was not an exceptional man. He was selfish and greedy, always looking for a chance to gain more in his pursuit of pleasure and the good life. But in every life, a moment comes when we have a chance to be more than what we have been. A time to rise up and do something that will be remembered and recounted. A moment when we realize that our lives are not as important as the call of the moment. Schindler rose above his old ways and found a way to be remembered with respect in history, despite his selfish greed and affiliation with the Nazis.

All because Schindler was asked, "What is a person worth to *you*?"

11

ME AND OSAMA ARE CLOSE

He who saves a life, saves the world entire.
—*From the film* Schindler's List

The life I touch for good or ill will touch another
life, and that in turn another, until who knows
where the trembling stops or in what far place my
touch will be felt?

—*Frederick Buechner*

Early in my attempts to develop leaders for church planting, I designed a ministry called the Pastor's Factory. Obviously this was before I started to see church from an organic point of view. At the time, I foolishly wanted to stamp out new leaders in a cookie-cutter manner.

I was mentoring an emerging leader named Barney. He had been in the Vietnam conflict and then in a biker gang, and now he was a concert promoter who turned his life over to Jesus. Barney is one of those larger-than-life dudes. He had many stories to tell, each of great interest and drama.

I gave an assignment to the Pastor's Factory students to develop a vision for reaching lost people. They were first to come up with the vision and then the strategy. Barney came to me very excited one afternoon with a plan that he said was sure to be powerful.

His idea was to hook up satellite signals so that a single broadcast could be shown around the world simultaneously on huge screens where mass populations could hear a concert and a Gospel presentation. "We could reach the whole world in one night, and then Jesus can return!"

Wow! Aside from the expense, translation challenges, and the logistical nightmare, I felt that he was shooting a little too high. I let him explain it all, and I couldn't help but share his enthusiasm, it was so contagious. It was very good to see his heart for the world.

After some time, I asked him a more pointed question: "Barney, has Sally come to know Christ yet?" (Sally was his wife.)

A little sheepish, he said, "No, not yet."

"How about your son?"

"Nah, still prayin' for him."

I said, "What do you say we pray about finding ways to present Christ to your own family first, and we take on global satellites a little further down the road?" He agreed that this was a better first step.

God has uniquely placed us all in relationships for the purpose of bringing Christ closer to people.

Six Degrees of God's Kingdom

In the mid-1990s three college students with a bottle of whiskey came up with a new game, which grew to become a cult fad. It is now so well known that even VISA commercials have capitalized on it. It is called Six Degrees of Kevin Bacon.

The idea of the game is to link any actor or actress, through the movies they have been in, to the actor Kevin Bacon in less than six steps. For instance, Kevin Bacon links to Kevin Costner in one swift link: both were in *JFK*. Julia Louis-Dreyfus of TV's "Seinfeld," however, takes all six steps to make a chain. She was in *Christmas Vacation* with Randy Quaid, who was in *Major League II* with Tom Berenger, who was in *Shattered* with Greta Scacchi, who was in *Presumed Innocent* with Harrison Ford, who was in *Raiders of the Lost Ark* with Karen Allen, who was in *Animal House* with Kevin Bacon.

There are actually Websites where you can sharpen your skills.[1] Brett Tjaden, a computer scientist at the University of Virginia, actually figured out the average number of jumps for more than 250,000 film actors to link to Kevin Bacon and came up with 2.8312 steps. In other words, every actor who has ever acted can be linked to Kevin Bacon in an average of just three steps.[2]

This game may be amusing, but the principle behind it is astounding. According to Dan Seligman in a *Forbes* article titled "Me and Monica," the average person has fifteen hundred acquaintances in life, with older and wealthier people tending to exceed that number. Our fifteen hundred acquaintances all begin to overlap in this world of 6.3 billion people. So the theory is that any two people on planet earth can be linked by five or fewer intermediaries.[3] Everybody is connected by only six degrees of separation. Unless of course you know my friend Carol Davis, in which case it is only two degrees of separation! It seems she knows everybody and makes the theory look even more reliable. In fact, it does work that way. There are certain people whom God has wired in such a way that they have an exceptional network of friends and associates. These key people actually reduce the distance of separation between many of us.[4]

The theory works like this: I know a guy who has a stepsister, whose cousin had a professor in college who once failed this fanatical man who knows where Osama Bin Laden is. Or something like that. Actually, you are only five or fewer links away from finding Jimmy Hoffa's body.

The CIA would be all over this, but the key is that you have to know the right six people or the chain does not work. Unfortunately, it is impossible for us to know who the right six people are to make any precise connection. But this does not mean the connection is not there; you just do not realize it. You are really only a jump or two from some of the most powerful or popular people in the world.

There is one Person who *does* know the links—all of them. God, in His infinite wisdom and grace, can connect the whole world to one another via a few simple relationships. This adds a whole new meaning to the phrase "It's a small world." Each person you meet is a doorway to a new world. We never know where this metaphorical door will open up to, but God sovereignly leads us to paths He has already preordained. We each have divinely ordained connections through relationships to reach the world. That is a great idea, and it has always been God's plan. The Gospel flies best on the wings of relationships.

However, normally when people want to reach a community for Christ, the church usually forms a committee to come up with some event aimed at attracting people to the church. Evangelistic events are not wrong, but I venture to say they are also not very effective at reaching people for the Kingdom.

I often take an unofficial survey when speaking to an audience. I ask people to raise their hand if they accepted Christ anonymously, without any relational witness of a respected friend. In other words, you heard a crowd in the stadium and thought the Yankees were playing. Amazed that they were not asking for tickets, you walked in and found it was a Billy Graham Crusade, and you got saved. Or you were going off to battle and a stranger handed you a Gideon's Bible, which you promptly put in your shirt pocket without another thought. In battle, a bullet struck you in your chest, but the Bible stopped it from ripping through your flesh and exploding in your heart. When you took out the Bible and opened it, you found the bullet stopped at John 3:16, which you read with renewed interest and got saved.

Perhaps a bit overdramatized, but stories like this are remarkable, and rare. When I ask people who have stories of anonymous salvation experiences apart from any friendly witness to raise their hand, usually only one or two do so.

Next, I ask people to raise their hand if they accepted Christ because of the faithful witness of a close friend, relative, or associate. The rest of the people always raise their hand. I ask, "So why are we so busy planning events to attract people when relationships are actually far more effective?"

The Gospel spread throughout the known world in the first century in a single generation. It did so through relationships—six degrees of relationships.

The word the New Testament often employs to describe our relational communities is the Greek *oikos*.[5] *Oikos* is in a family of words based on the idea of home or household. It is used to refer to the houses people live in and the homes that churches meet in, as well as the fact that believers all belong to the household of God. But the usage goes beyond a house with a white picket fence or the nuclear family. At times, a person's *oikos* is the fundamental natural unit of society: one's family, friends, neighbors, and associates.

Cornelius is instructed by the Lord to gather his household together to hear the Gospel from Peter (in Acts 10:22–27). When Peter arrived, it was not just Cornelius' immediate family. It says that he entered a large room filled with people. It included Cornelius' family, relatives, slaves, associates, and neighbors—his *oikos*.

In much of the world, an *oikos* is literally a person's household or family. Many cultures, particularly more rural ones, have a family as the basic unit of society. In more urban and suburban societies, people do not build their social lives around family but instead around homogeneous interests. A person's *oikos* may not consist of blood relatives but of people who share common interests, hobbies, or employment.

Oikos is one's social web of relationships. It can take the Gospel to some incredible places, as the Lord of the harvest does what only He can do.

While in prison in Rome, Paul wrote to the Philippians to let them know that his imprisonment had not hindered the spread of the Gospel (Phil. 1:12). Amazingly enough, it actually opened doors to new worlds of relationships that led even to Caesar's palace. Some of Caesar's own *oikos* in Rome as well became believers (Phil. 4:22). Because Paul was locked up with a Roman guard, he instantly had only two degrees of separation from the most powerful leader in the world. God used that to bring salvation even to Nero's own family.

In the sermons Jesus gave teaching us how to start the Kingdom epidemic, He used *oikos* as the context for the spread. In Luke 10:5–7, He said (*oikos*, translated as "house," is in italics for emphasis): "When you enter a *house*, first say, 'Peace to this *house*.' If a man of peace is there, your peace will rest on him; if not, it will return to you. Stay in that *house*, eating and drinking whatever they give you, for the worker deserves his wages. Do not move around from *house* to *house*."

The Lord of the Harvest has directed us to the *oikos* to spread the Kingdom of God. This is, in fact, the way of spreading the Gospel most often put forth in the New Testament. It appears that the Lord of the harvest has indeed set us up in a particular *oikos* to reach people who do not know Him yet.

Paul spoke to an audience of Greek philosophers and brought great enlightenment to God's intentional influence through the six degrees of separation on a global scale. He said:

> The God who made the world and everything in it is the Lord of heaven and earth and does not live in temples built by hands. And he is not served by human hands, as if he needed anything, because he himself gives all men life and breath and everything else. From one man he made every nation of men, that they should inhabit the whole earth; and he determined the times set for them and the exact places where they should live. God did this so that men would seek him and perhaps reach out for him and find him, though he is not far from each one of us [Acts 17:25–27].

The Scriptures tell us that God intentionally placed us in certain relational contexts by His providence. He did so that we may be close to finding Him. It makes sense that this is God's design to reach the world.

I was once asked to speak at Fuller Seminary about developing leaders for missions and church planting. This was the first time I was presented with such an opportunity, so I was honored, even a little full of myself. During the day, I received a message from a relative that her son, Jerald, lay dying in the hospital, and she wanted to know if I would go visit with him. I barely knew him, but we were family. Being the only pastor in the family, I was the obvious one for her to call in a moment like this.

The problem was that I received the call late in the day and was on the other side of Los Angeles on a Friday afternoon. The traffic would be unbearable. I decided that I just wanted to go home, so I did not want to return the call. I would call the next day. On my way to the car, however, the Holy Spirit had another idea. He began to show me that I would drive all this way to speak about evangelism, but that I was not willing to drive far to actually do the work. Ouch! I got the point, and I called my relative.

The drive turned out to be only twenty-five minutes, which seemed miraculous to me. It was grace abounding where sin did once abound. I visited Jerald and stayed for almost an hour. He was unable to communicate. I was not even sure he could hear me, but I read the entire Gospel of Mark to him and led him in a prayer to welcome Jesus as his King and Savior. Whether he heard me or understood, I do not know; I leave such things to the Savior. Then I went home, grateful that the Holy Spirit would not leave me in my selfish ways. The traffic was still miraculously light.

But this was not the end of the story. A week later, I received another call. Jerald had passed away, and I was asked to lead his memorial service at the beach. It happened to be at the very beach where I used to be a lifeguard. More than a hundred people came to remember Jerald, and I was able to share the Good News of the Kingdom with a hundred people I would never have met in the normal course of life. Two lifeguards I used to work with daily and had not seen in some years also stood by and listened. It was a shock for them to see someone they used to see every day on the beach in a whole new light.

The call I received that Friday afternoon when I was not alert to spiritual things was to come and share not just with one dying man but with more than a hundred dying souls. Each person is a door for the Kingdom to enter into a new *oikos*. This same relative has already had me share at two other funerals, to hundreds of others. God sees these connections, and we do not; this is why we must move forward in faith and obedience. We may stumble upon something incredible if we do.

A Relational Kingdom

If a changed life is the result and the contagion of the Kingdom, then of course a relational community is the best place for the Kingdom to spread. The changed life is most noticed by those who know the new convert.

If we examine the New Testament, we see how quickly the Gospel spreads from *oikos* to *oikos*. Several examples all describe the spread of the Gospel through relations in the context of a person's *oikos* in the book of Acts. In each case, the Gospel infected a whole household or *oikos*: Cornelius (Acts 10:2; 11:13–15); Lydia (Acts 16:15); the Philippian jailer (Acts 16:31–34); and Crispus, the leader of the Synagogue in Corinth (Acts 18:7–9).

This idea is not only the way Jesus prescribed for us to reach the world; it is also His own practice. He leads by example. His own cousin (John the Baptist) introduced Jesus to Andrew, who then brought his brother Simon (later called Peter) to Jesus. Peter was instrumental in bringing James and John Zebedee to Christ. They all became part of the core team of leaders Jesus mentored for a global movement of the Kingdom. It began in His own *oikos* and spread via other people's *oikos*. Jesus had the capability to reach masses in events that would put our own efforts to shame, but He always shied away from mass outreach and invested in *oikos* relationships that could multiply and spread.

The keys to evangelism as practiced in churches today have focused on creative turns of a phrase to bring a conversation to the Gospel or correct answers to defend our beliefs. In Jesus' pattern, relationships are the context, and the keys to sharing are quite different. Within the context of our *oikos*, these are the keys to being a strong witness:

- *Time and availability.* Relationships that are significant take time. One of the reasons our evangelism is often minimally effective is because we are more interested in rationally conveying a message than we are at truly getting to know people and letting them know us.
- *A transformed life.* The new life we have in Christ is contagious. This is what the world is dying to have and rarely gets to see.
- *Hospitality.* Our changed life and kingdom values will best be seen in our everyday life. Practicing hospitality is a powerful way to bridge into deeper relationships where others can see our life in Christ.
- *Spiritual intuition.* This requires listening carefully, to others and to the Holy Spirit. Rather than relying on a canned presentation of the Gospel that is used every time, listen to others and to the promptings of God's Spirit and you will see more fruit in evangelism. Everybody is unique, and the Spirit knows what the core longings of each person's soul are.
- *Generosity.*[6] There are few character traits that stand out in this world more than a generous heart. People are drawn to someone who gives freely and cheerfully.

A Great Paradox: The Easiest and the Hardest Channel for the Gospel

Although God has made the *oikos* the most natural setting in which to be a witness, it can also be a difficult spiritual environment, particularly for those who have been believers for a long time. Jesus said, "A prophet is not without honor except in his hometown and among his own relatives and in his own household" (Mark 6:4). Sometimes our own relatives are the hardest to reach. Jesus Himself had to rise from the dead to convince His brothers of His true identity. It may take something dramatic for their hearts to be open to our story of redemption. Pray, and God will do things for our family members that we cannot.

If we can begin to see the Gospel spread relationally, then the new believer's dramatic change of life will be a strong witness in their *oikos*. Some of us need to look to the *oikos* of others rather than our own. We can pray and hope that one day God will do something dramatic to open the hearts of our own family and relatives, much as He did in Jesus' own *oikos*. I do not suggest that we wait for a great response from our own *oikos*. As you move on to another *oikos*, you are not abandoning your family; you are leaving them in better hands. You will know when the right time comes to renew your witness. While you wait for God to soften hearts in your own family, you might as well be looking for other opportunities to relationally bring the Kingdom to other *oikos*.

Usually the pattern is that either your own family is transformed soon after your own salvation or it takes a lifetime. In either case, God loves your family and will pursue them.

I grew up in a home that did not have any faith in God. When I was a small boy, a neighborhood friend became a Christian. I distinctly remember my mother pulling me aside and telling me, "Neil, don't you ever become a Jesus freak like Ricky." So when I became a follower of Christ in my freshman year of college, I found it difficult to tell my family, especially my mother. It took me a year to come out and tell the truth. I drove home from college with a stack of books, all defending the rationality of the Christian faith. I placed the stack on the coffee table in the living room in front of both my parents and my uncle and announced, "I have become a Christian, and these books will explain why you should too." I was surprised to hear my mother say, "Oh, we knew you became a Christian."

My family wasn't ready to put their faith in Christ at that time, and no amount of books would change things. But they were prepared to start watching me, and for a few years they watched. They saw me get married. They watched our marriage. They saw me graduate from college and start seminary.

I prayed every day for my parents, and it seemed as though none of the prayers were getting past the ceiling. My mother was very proud, and I thought she would be the last person to ever accept Jesus. I remember praying for the Lord to do whatever it takes to save her soul. A short time later I learned that she had an advanced form of cancer, and she started an aggressive treatment.

One evening, while still in my lifeguard uniform from a long day of work, I stopped by to see my mother before going home. We were talking about my day and her medical treatment when she surprised me with a straightforward question: "Who do you take after?" I said, "Well, you and dad are the only parents I have ever had, so I guess you both." She said, "No, you're not like me, and you're nothing like your father. What makes you so different from the way you were brought up?" "That's Jesus," I replied. "You're seeing Jesus in my life; that's the only explanation."

We then went into a long talk about who Jesus truly is and what the Gospel is all about. Before I knew it the sun was rising. We had talked all through the night. Within a few weeks, she became a follower of Christ.

At one point, close to her death, she sat up in bed with perfect clarity and said goodbye to the whole family. Then she asked me to read the last chapter of the Bible. She said, "I don't have time to read the whole thing, so I just want to hear if it has a good ending." She also wanted the rest of the family to hear the ending as well, and to know that her newfound faith was real. I read the last chapter, and she lay back down and fell into the effects of the painkillers.

A short time later, my mother died. My father has yet to accept Christ, and it has been more than twenty years. Sometimes our changed life has an immediate result in our *oikos*; sometimes it takes a lifetime. But it is always the transformed life of Christ in us that makes the difference.

12

THE HOW-TO OF SPREADING THE EPIDEMIC

What lies behind us and what lies before us are tiny matters compared to what lies within us.
—*Ralph Waldo Emerson*

Be the change you want to see in the world.
—*Mahatma Gandhi*

I once read a story of two men who saw an advertisement placed by local farmers who were tired of having their livestock eaten by a pack of wolves. The ad offered $500 per wolf, taken dead or alive. The two entrepreneurs set off with their camping supplies and rifles. After a couple of days of fruitless hunting, the two collapsed in fatigue by a warm campfire they had built. Hearing a noise, one awoke, only to notice the glow of fire reflecting off the eyes and teeth of a pack of hungry wolves surrounding their little camp. He slowly, yet urgently, reached over to nudge his partner awake. In a hushed and frantic voice he whispered, "Jerry! Jerry, wake up! *We're RICH!*"

Perspective can change the way we see our surroundings. Perspective is the difference between fear and courage. A little kid, walking home from school, is confronted by the neighborhood bully. He runs but to no avail. He stumbles and falls to the ground as the bully approaches with threatening words and snarls, "I'm gonna pulverize you!" Unbeknownst to the bully, the boy's big brother from college comes up behind the bully. If the boy looks at the bully, he may feel fear. But if he chooses to look at the brother, he may lose his fear and even feel cocky and calm. The difference is perspective.

Perspective, then, is what tells us we are secure despite the environment we are in. Perspective can see an ominous situation as a great opportunity.

Jesus said, "Behold, I send you out as sheep in the midst of wolves" (Luke 10:16). In this same passage, He referred to sheep more than once. He mentioned "sheep without a shepherd," "lost sheep of the house of Israel," and then "sheep in the midst of the wolves." The first two comments refer to pitiful, broken sheep that are helpless and hopeless. The third comment doesn't. In this comment, Jesus, the Chief Shepherd, actually sends us sheep into the very den of the wolves.

What kind of a shepherd does that?! Why would the Good Shepherd send us to the wolves?

Perhaps it is because these are special sheep. Perhaps we are considered a strange new breed of sheep: teenage-mutant-ninja sheep with super powers.

No, the difference is not in the sheep as much as the Shepherd. We all need reminding at times that we are no different from the lost sheep except that we now have a Shepherd—and what a difference He makes. We do not need to fear the pack of wolves because He is with us, carries a big stick, and has a quick swing. Wherever we go, the Shepherd goes.

So why are we sent to the wolves? Though He is our protection, He is also on a mission to seek and save the lost sheep, and the wolves tend to gather where there is easy prey.

Jesus was sent to seek. Those who follow Him are also sent to seek (John 20:21). As disciples of Christ we have gone from being vulnerable prey to becoming valued members of a search-and-rescue team. The Great Shepherd is willing to go into the den of wolves to rescue one sheep from the jaws of a hungry wolf.

This is not a safe calling, but a worthy one. It is not always comfortable to be amid wolves. Is Jesus interested in our comfort? Of course He is; that is why He sent us His Comforter. Our comfort, however, is not to come from safe surroundings but from a source of strength within. This strength is most evident in distressing scenarios, even when we are surrounded by the wolves.

Note that the difference is not in the sheep but the presence of the Shepherd. That is all it takes to go from being the hunted to the hunter. This is true for all followers of Jesus. When we face our bully, we have a big Brother who will be our strength, our defense. If our perspective is right, we have no need to run in fear.

Jesus' Plan to Spread the Kingdom

In these highly practical messages from Jesus, found in both Matthew 10 and Luke 10, we can uncover five principles that help us start churches that will reproduce. They all have the acronym POP so that they are easy to remember and pass on to others.

Practice of Prayer

In both sermons, Jesus begins with familiar words: "The harvest is plentiful but the laborers are few. Therefore beseech the Lord of the harvest to send out workers into the harvest" (Luke 10:2; Matt. 10:38). We believe that church is a spiritual entity before it is a physical reality. Remember, the Church is conceived in heaven before it is born on earth. It must first be a glimmer in our Father's eyes.

We begin churches by wooing the Bridegroom for new workers to come out of the harvest. The Groom is easily wooed by the bride (as are most grooms) because He wants the church to reproduce more than we do. This is His idea. Church planting is a great spiritual romance that involves intimacy, courting, and reproduction. Many experts have reduced it to demographic research, strategic planning, job descriptions, and organizational flow charts. How romantic!

We simply cannot skip this important part of church planting. Jesus began both sermons with the same appeal: "Beseech the Lord of the harvest for workers." We are to beg, beseech, and plead with God for these workers. The word used for "pray" (in the King James

Version) means to beg as if for mercy, as if for your life (Luke 21:36; Acts 8:22; 2 Cor. 5:20).

There is no substitute for going out among the lost people, looking deep into their eyes, and begging God for their souls. Of course, the Lord of the harvest longs to answer these prayers. He bled so that these souls could be saved.

It is in the prayer that the romantic part of church planting is introduced. This is very important to the church, to the Father, and to the community we want to reach. It is when we are in deep intercession for freedom of souls that we are closest to the heart of God. This is the spiritual intimacy that tears down strongholds of the enemy and builds new life in its place. This is the first step in starting churches that reproduce. Pray first, pray last, and in between pray hard.

The prayer that Jesus suggests is a simple idea, but then again the best ideas are usually simple. Beg God for workers, obeying Luke 10:2B. A prayer movement started in Denver, Colorado, with some good friends, John White and Kenny Moore. They infected me with the bug. I mention it now almost everywhere I go. Others do as well. We now commonly refer to this idea as the 10:2B virus. Every morning at 10:02 A.M. my electronic organizer is programmed to have an alarm go off and remind me to beg God for more laborers.

I started praying the 10:2B prayer in December 2003. At that time our association had only forty-two church planters. By late January 2004 we had more than eighty. Less than a year postinfection, the consequences of the 10:2B virus are a one hundred increase in church planters.

Why should we expect anything else? This is Jesus' idea. He wants to answer the prayers even more than we want them answered. He is the one who said, "Ask and you shall receive."

This virus is now spreading. Now you have been infected. Take Jesus at His word. Ask Him for more souls. Thousands of years before my friends started spreading the virus, Jesus first instigated the plan. Make a daily practice of begging God for souls and for workers for the harvest, from the harvest. The Lord of the harvest will not disappoint you.

Pockets of People

Jesus instructed His disciples not to go the way of the Gentiles or the Samaritans but specifically the way of the lost sheep of the house of Israel (Matt. 10:5). He sent the disciples out in pairs to various cities and villages looking for a pocket of people, a community of lost souls who were receptive to the message of peace (Luke 10:1). He taught the disciples to spot a receptive *oikos*.

When looking for a pocket of people remember the saying that bad people make good soil—there's a lot of fertilizer in their lives.

People are tribal by nature and always have been. From the beginning, God said, "It is not good for man to be alone" (Gen. 2:18). Those who find themselves truly alone are the ones who take their own lives or do terrible things to engage with others.

After just a few months of hanging out at that first coffeehouse, I had my living room full of new believers. The coffeehouse was transformed by the Gospel. Rather than follow traditional church planting theory and move into a larger location, we sent a small team to a new coffeehouse.

The second coffeehouse, called Portfolios, was a much darker and more sinister place. A witch's coven would hang out there each night. There were warlocks, Satanists, and vampires. I'd never even heard of vampires before (other than the fictitious ones like Dracula). But there is a subculture of people here in California who actually live a strange life based on the writings and mythological culture of vampires. Some file their teeth to become fangs. Some sleep in coffins, drink blood, drive hearses, and come out only at night. Some also practice black magic and cast spells on people.

The first person to become a Christian at Portfolios was Manuel. Tim, one of our team members, was an excellent evangelist. He sat across the table from Manuel and opened his Bible to Romans 6:23; he gave it to Manuel to read for himself. Just then Joey, a recruiter for the occult and part of the coven, came and sat next to Manuel. Joey likes to talk and has a foul mouth, so Tim prayed silently, "Lord, keep his ears open and his mouth closed." Joey didn't say a word.

Then Jack came and sat on the other side of Manuel. Jack is an atheist philosopher who loves to talk but doesn't ever get very far. Tim prayed the same silent prayer, and Jack didn't say a word.

Finally, "Psycho Saul" came up behind Tim. Psycho Saul is the leader of the vampires. He is tall, thin, and pale, and he dresses all in black with a long black trench coat and long frizzy hair down his back. Saul leaned over and whispered to Tim, "I just want you to know that I have my sword with me." Tim answered, "Oh, that's nice; I have mine too," pointing to his Bible. "Manuel is reading it now." Then Psycho Saul leaned over again and said, "No. I really do have my sword." And he opened his trench coat and there, hanging from his belt, was a real double-edged sword. Tim prayed silently again, "Lord, keep his ears open and his mouth closed, and don't let him cut my head off." One thing I know about Tim is that he is not easily intimidated. This only helped him to focus more on the opportunity that the Lord had placed before him.

Manuel glanced up from his reading at that moment with a confused look on his face. He read it again, and suddenly the lights went on in his eyes and a smile came across his face. He understood that the wages of his sin was death, "but the gift of God is eternal life in Christ Jesus, our Lord." At that moment, Joey got up to leave. Jack rose from the table and walked away, and Psycho Saul took his sword and left.

From that moment, Portfolios became holy ground. Manuel was baptized at the beach within a week. Within a few weeks he was baptizing his first convert at the same beach. He baptized another convert a few weeks after that. Within a short time a second church was started from converts from Portfolios. Then, a short time later a third was started out of the rich, dark soil of this pocket of people.

In our experience, coffeehouses have proven to be fertile soil for the gospel. Now, however, we have expanded our vision to other arenas as well. We have churches that reach out to twelve-step recovery groups, neighborhood gangs, homosexuals, occult groups, high schools, college and university campuses, the homeless, and local bars. The key is not in the building but in bringing the Kingdom of God to the people He is calling out. In searching for a fertile pocket of people, look for a strong sense of community and social cohesiveness. Just like the bar Cheers in the TV show of the same name, look for a place "where everybody knows your name."

Jesus' plan is for us to identify a pocket of people who do not have a vital Kingdom witness. Then we enter into relationship with those people. We inject the Kingdom virus right into the darkness, and a church is born there from the changed lives. If they are not receptive (which happens frequently), we simply wipe the dust (bad soil) off our feet and move on to the next pocket of people.

Luke tells us that the disciples were sent to go to the places where He Himself was about to come (Luke 10:1). Though this was literal, I cannot help but see it in a spiritual sense as well. We are looking for the places where His Spirit is telling us that Jesus is going to come. Like Moses, I made a commitment when I first set off in this church planting adventure that I would not go where He Himself was not going. In other words, I would not be willing to go if He did not go too, and the moment I sensed it was me planting the church rather than Him I would call it quits. This is my commitment to this very day.

A spiritual sensitivity to the places and ways in which the Lord of the harvest is working is crucial for anyone wanting to serve the Lord. As Henry Blackaby teaches, we should find out what God is doing and join Him.[1] To do ministry any other way is just sad.

Power of Presence

Jesus told the disciples as He sent them out that they had authority to do the works of God. He said: "As you go, preach this message: 'The kingdom of heaven is near.' Heal the sick, raise the dead, cleanse those who have leprosy, drive out demons. Freely you have received, freely give" (Matt. 10:7–8).

They were to announce that the Kingdom of God has come near, whether they were received or not (Luke 10:10–12).

We have another saying in our churches: "Where you go, the King goes, and where the King goes, people bow." In the Great Commission, Jesus said these words: "All authority in heaven and earth has been given to me" (Matt. 28:18). That's a lot of authority. In fact, it is *all* authority. There is no door that Jesus cannot unlock and open. He is the One who "opens the door and no one can shut it" (Rev. 3:7).

When I was a kid, we used to have a travel game called Connect the Dots. By connecting each dot in the proper order, even the least creative person can become an instant artist. I want you to connect the dots in the Great Commission mentioned in Matthew 28:18–20. Jesus begins with this: "All authority in Heaven and Earth is with me." He ends with "I am with you." Now connect the dots: all power of heaven and earth goes with you wherever you go. Wow. That is something to consider.

C. H. Spurgeon, the great preacher of nineteenth-century England, was once preaching on this passage and made an observation that is worth repeating: "You have a factor here that is absolutely infinite, and what does it matter what other factors may be? 'I will do the best I can' says one. Any fool can do that. He that believes in Christ does what he cannot do, attempts the impossible and performs it."

We must not forget this. The enemy is hoping that we will not realize this important truth, because he is vulnerable to us when we learn it. Jesus' promise is for all who follow Him.

One night at Portfolios, my friend Tim caught a vampire behind his back doing something suspicious with his hands. He was casting an evil spell on Tim. Concerned about this, Tim later asked a friend who was in the occult what it meant. "The vampires have a spell they do to people they don't like," his friend explained. "They walk up behind their victims and suck the spirit out of them." When Tim shared this with me, my initial response was, "Let him suck away; he'll never thirst again!"

Of course, that's not really the way to taste from the spring of Living Water, but I have no fear of such curses because I *do* have a spring of eternal life within me that is greater than any curse. My curse was taken on the cross (Gal. 3:13). "Greater is He that is in [me] than he that is in the world!" (1 John 4:4).

Someone once asked Tim what the secret was to seeing so many people come to Christ. His answer was simple: "Two words: show up." Non-Christians aren't fretting, trying to figure out ways to get into church. Church is not something they feel they need or want, or are even curious about. So often we erect a difficult barrier to evangelism by expecting people to come to our churches to find Christ. Many non-Christians have more problems with church than with Christ, so we make their salvation that much more difficult.

There is another notion we often repeat in our movement. There are two kinds of lost people in the world, the moths and the cockroaches. In the darkness, it's impossible to tell them apart, so the best way to discover the difference is to turn the light on. The moths will be drawn to the light, and the cockroaches will flee.

Jesus told us that we are a light that should not be hidden even behind stained-glass windows (Matt. 5:14–16). Most of us don't turn all the lights on in our home during the day. Why? A lamp isn't needed during the daylight. Light is made for the darkness. "You are the light of the world" (Matt. 5:14). We should be brought out into the darkness so that we can shine.

Jesus also noted that the disciples were not to import resources into the harvest but to find all the resources they needed in the harvest itself. He instructed the disciples: "Do not take a purse or bag or sandals; and do not greet anyone on the road. When you enter a house, first say, 'Peace to this house.' If a man of peace is there, your peace will rest on him; if not, it will return to you. Stay in that house, eating and drinking whatever they give you, for the worker deserves his wages. Do not move around from house to house" (Luke 10:4–7).

When you enter a town and are welcomed, eat what is set before you. His instructions were to not bring any extra clothes, food, or money to sustain the ministry. This is crucial. Too often we set up impossible standards for church life by importing resources that the indigenous church could never meet on its own. We create a codependent relationship, which is unhealthy and nonreproductive.

Our resources are to be found first in Christ Himself and second in the harvest.

When Jesus said "the harvest is plentiful" this was meant as good news. Still, we read it as bad news, because it means that there are so many lost and dying people in the world. This is true, but if you were to tell a farmer that his harvest is plentiful he would rejoice at the good news, and so should we. The good news is not that so many are lost and dying, but that so many are going to be saved once we start taking the power of the Kingdom into their world. All the resources needed for a great harvest are already found in the harvest itself—finances, facilities, future leaders. All we need is to get out there and reap. There is much power in showing up. We neglect to remember the profound power found in just the story of "Christ and Him crucified." We underestimate how powerful His resurrection is.

The first coffeehouse we started visiting was completely transformed in a short time. I will never forget sitting across a chess board from a troubled young man who had once tried to take his own life. As we spoke, he confessed that he understood the reality of hell and was deathly afraid of going there. As I spoke with him about the Kingdom of God, both here now and in the future, we started to hear heavenly music. We both chuckled. One of our church members had a guitar and started playing across the patio. Others joined in and spontaneously a worship service broke loose at the Coffee Tavern. Everyone was singing or listening. One of the gentlemen we had been reaching out to started translating the songs into sign language. It was beautiful. The dark place had become full of light. This experience also helped open the eyes of a young man who felt powerless and hopeless in life.

Every person at this coffeehouse either was born again or left. Once that happened, we all decided to move to another coffeehouse where there was more good soil. Although we never intended for it to happen, the old coffeehouse went out of business and had to be reopened later under new ownership. The Kingdom of God is a powerful and transforming presence.

This same power became evident at our next coffeehouse, Port-folios. One night a few years after we first broke into the *oikos* of Portfolios, I was there with some interns who were preparing to go to Portland, Oregon. We were discussing spiritual things with an-other occultist named J. T., who was being groomed for leadership of that movement. He was convinced that in the end of times he would be riding the white horse of the apocalypse. I politely dis-agreed. In the course of our conversation, J. T. casually mentioned that all the occultists had mutually decided that Portfolios was now neutral territory and that no one was allowed to cast any more spells there.

He didn't understand why I started laughing, so I enlightened him. I said, "You know perfectly well that Portfolios is not neutral territory!" He countered, "Oh, yes it is. We all decided." "No," I an-swered, "you decided you can't cast any spells here anymore because this is now God's territory. This is sacred ground now, and your spells don't work." J. T. continued to object to my commentary until we were interrupted by Sean, who brought a friend up to me and said, "This is Jorge, and he wants to accept Jesus right here, right now." I told Sean, "You know what to do." Right in front of this oc-cultist, while he was still claiming Portfolios as neutral territory, Jorge got on his knees and entered the Kingdom of God.

Person of Peace

The fourth principle is one that I am indebted to my dear friend and mentor Thom Wolf for uncovering. This simple concept has led to many churches being born around the world. Jesus said to look for and even inquire about someone who would be receptive to our message of peace. When we find such a person, we are to stay there and reach his or her entire household (*oikos*). We are to eat what he or she eats and stay where he or she stays (Luke 10:6–7).

If you saw a human hand sticking up out of the sand waving for help at the beach, you would make an obvious assumption: there is a body attached to that hand and it needs air. When a person comes to believe and follow Christ, we do not just add another member to an existing body. Three hands might be helpful at times, but it would certainly not be natural. When someone believes, we assume that he or she is a part of a body yet to be uncovered. We assume that God would not want a child of God to be alone, so there must be others that He is intending to save as well. We keep digging until the body emerges and is whole and healthy.

When someone comes to Christ in a new pocket of people, we assume that this is a person of peace. It doesn't always turn out that way, but the assumption is helpful. More often than not the assumption is true.

Persons of peace are characterized by three things:

1. *They are people of receptivity.* They are open to the message of the person and the peace of Christ.

2. *They are people of relational connections.* They know lots of people and are an important part of the community, for better or worse.

3. *They are people of reputation.* They possess a reputation, whether it is good or bad.

The person of peace becomes the conduit for the passing of the message of the Kingdom to an entire community of lost people. The person's reputation gives credence to the message and becomes a magnet for a new church. A poor reputation can often be the catalyst for a dynamic church as the whole community sees the life-transforming power of Jesus.

Here are some examples of persons of peace in the New Testament. I call them the "first domino" people, who start a chain reaction for the Kingdom. When they became Christian, others within the *oikos* did so as well, often almost immediately. You will see that some were people of good reputation, and others had a bad reputation.

Lydia was a woman of good reputation. She was the seller of purple fabric, which was considered quite valuable. In Philippi, she was a well-respected businesswoman. When Paul and Silas found her near the river, they told her about Jesus and she became a follower, as did all her household or *oikos*.

The Samaritan woman at the well in John 4 had a reputation, but not a good one. There is a reason she was down at the well during the hot afternoon when no one else would be there. As Jesus informs us, she had five husbands in her past, and the guy she was now hooked up with wasn't her husband at all. After she came to believe in Jesus as the Messiah, she brought her whole village to Jesus.

Cornelius had a good reputation with all men. When Peter brought the Gospel to him, his entire social web of relations (*oikos*) came to Christ (Acts 11:11–18).

The Gerasene Demoniac is my favorite example of a New Testament person of peace sent out to reach his own *oikos*. People say first impressions are important. The first impression one might have had meeting this man is that he was naked! Upon further investigation, it was clear he had problems. His hair was matted, his long fingernails were dirty, and he had a wild look in his eyes. When he spoke, a thousand voices came out, saying, "We are Legion for we are many." To me those are some of the most terrifying words in the Bible. Can you imagine the stories high school kids told about this guy? The urban legend must have been dramatic. Imagine the dares that fraternity pledges had to go through as a hazing that might involve this guy.

Jesus cast out the demons from this man. They entered a herd of pigs who commit "swine-i-cide," or you might say, "Su-eee-cide." Some call this the first case of "deviled ham."

Well, granted, my own sense of humor may be lame, but I am constantly reminded that the Bible does have a good sense of humor. It says that the man was then fully dressed and in his right mind, sitting at Jesus' feet, "and then the people became frightened" (Mark 5:15). I can't help but laugh at that verse. When he was breaking chains with his bare hands, streaking naked to live in the tombs with dead corpses, the people were fine. Once he was fully clothed and sane, *then* they were afraid!

This fear propelled the people to send Jesus away. Being a gentleman, Jesus would never force Himself on anyone, so He stepped back into the boat. The formerly demon-possessed man asked Jesus to take him along. Jesus did not allow him to come; instead, He sent him out, saying, "Go home to your people" (Mark used the word "house," or *oikos*) "and report to them what great things the Lord has done for you, and how He had mercy on you." Mark goes on to describe that "he went away and began to proclaim in Decapolis what great things Jesus had done for him; and everyone marveled" (Mark 5:19, 20).

The man was a freak, yet God sent him to a place called Decapolis (which means "ten cities"). He had been saved for only ten minutes, and now he was a missionary to ten cities. I have trouble with only one city, and I have been a believer for more than twenty years. He had not taken a newcomers' class, had not been through the discipleship curriculum, and did not even know his spiritual gift profile yet, but he was sent to ten cities. Dare I mention that perhaps the fellow had a few issues to work out? A few minutes with Jesus was all it took. Amazing! If any one of us were to do this, we would be considered irresponsible. But Jesus did it.

Was the man effective? The next time Jesus went through that region, people were no longer afraid of Him. Probably because this man's reputation was so well known (both before and after), thousands came to meet Jesus and brought their sick, their demonized, and their handicapped. Jesus not only healed them all but fed them too (Mark 7:31–8:10; cf. Matt. 15:29–38).

Just a couple weeks after Manuel was baptized at the beach, he was baptizing his first convert at that same beach. A few weeks later, he was baptizing his second convert.

Over and over again, God proves this principle to be true and valued in transforming lives.

People of Purpose

The final principle for starting an epidemic is a people of purpose. Jesus instructs us that when a pocket of people receive your message of peace via a person of peace, it will rest upon them, and they become the church in their own rich soil (Matt. 10:11–13).

When the moths are drawn to the light and the person of peace brings several to Christ, a church is born. This is the formation of a people of purpose, born in the harvest, born *for* the harvest of neighborhoods and nations. Often, though not exclusively, the person of peace has the church meet in his or her home and may even be the new leader of the emerging church.

A church that starts this way is unique in that it is born out of the harvest, is found among the harvest, and is bent on a mission to continue to reach the lost. This missional element, inherent in each one's life-changing salvation, is the important drive to reach out and reproduce spontaneously. Many house churches suffer from "koinonitis," where fellowship and community is the main and only thing. What is needed is a strong, healthy dose of mission from the beginning.

Churches that start this way are unhindered by cultural Christianity, because they are born in the harvest. There is a simple purity to them that doesn't have the stain of the more placid and established Christendom. These people learn how to reach their friends from the start and don't know any better than to follow Jesus and expect Him to save their family, friends, and ultimately nations. They become a people of purpose, a spiritual family called out by God on a mission.

The first year and a half of my own church plant was exciting. Being with all-new converts who were fresh to following Christ was rejuvenating and refreshing. Granted, we had dirty diapers to attend to, but there was such *life*.

One week, I was away in Europe doing some training when a small band of students from a Midwestern Christian college came to visit our church. They saw what this sort of new life looked and felt like, where everyone was sharing Christ with friends, relatives, and neighbors.

When I returned to my church, I asked how the visit went. Michelle said, "Oh, it was fine. Y'know, that was the first time I ever met any 'real' Christians." The look on her face was less than enthusiastic.

I asked, "So what did you think of real Christians?"

"Hmm, well, they were nice."

"But . . . ?"

"Well, they didn't seem very excited about Jesus," was her honest appraisal.

Later that winter, I happened to be speaking at that same Christian college, so the students who had visited Awakening in my absence asked me out to breakfast. At breakfast, one of the students blew me away with his comment in describing what they saw: "That was the first time I ever met what I would call *real* Christians." This student and Michelle had both used the same language, but the contrast was obvious.

It is common for new Christians to lead their friends to Christ in our church and baptize new converts. Reading the Bible extensively is something everybody does. Confession of sin is a regular part of everyone's Christian walk in our church. To college kids who grew up in a Midwestern church, I am sure this was the first time they had ever really encountered believers similar to ones described in the New Testament. But it does not have to be that way.

Instead of drawing people *out* of community and robbing what community already existed, Jesus' plan is to inject the Gospel into an existing community. Like a virus, the peace of the Good News infects and transforms the community so that the members become a church themselves.

Most people setting out to start new churches automatically think of starting in their own home, but Jesus' idea of starting in the home of the new converts is a small shift with global implications. I suggest that if it takes a little longer to find an open home, it is worth the wait rather than starting in your own home. Trust Jesus' plan. He felt it was a strong enough plan to repeat it.

Contrast the Conventional Approach with Jesus' Plan

I once saw a cartoon of an old man explaining evangelism to a young couple. He said, "When I was a kid we used to run up to a neighbor's door, ring the bell, and run away. Now we call that visitation." I would like for you to imagine how Jesus' plan can actually work out in a neighborhood in your community.

The traditional approach to outreach is that you go to the neighborhood, knock on the first door, and pray that no one is home. If anyone is there, good, but if no one is there, you feel relieved. Then you knock on the next door. If some one is there, you talk.

Imagine, in a best-case scenario, you go to the third door and find a single mother struggling to make ends meet with two or three jobs. She feels weighed down with guilt and concern for her kids, and she is lonely. She hears your message of hope and a relationship with Jesus, and she accepts Him. What you do next with her is the difference between a church planting movement and just church growth. Usually you would take her six blocks away to where the church is and ask her to become a part of your community. In so doing, you have added one member to your church.

In Matthew 10, Jesus instructs us to use another strategy. You go to the first door, knock, and hope no one is home (you are still human). A friendly but cautious man comes to the door. After you talk with him, you find that he is not really interested in the Gospel.

What do you do next, according to Jesus' plan? You do not just go next door; you ask the man a question. Jesus said, "When you come into a town, inquire who is worthy in it" (Matt. 10:11). His idea is genius. You ask the non-Christians who the people are in the community who need to hear the message most, and they will help you start a church.

What does Jesus mean by "who is worthy"? Later in the same chapter Jesus defines it for us: "He who loves father or mother more than me is not worthy of me" (Matt. 10:37). In other words, it is someone desperate enough to give up everything for Christ. So you ask the people in the house, "Is there anyone here in this community who really needs to hear this message?" The man says, "Yes, four houses down, that guy is partying all night. The music is loud late into the night. There are always beer bottles all over his front lawn. Please go save that guy so I can get some sleep." You will find that even self-righteous unbelievers who are not interested some-how intuitively know the people who will be open to your message of hope and peace. They often try to help.

Now you do *not* go next door; instead, you go four doors down, step over the beer bottles, and knock on the door.

A burly guy in a white tank top that is stretched thin around a large beer gut comes to the door. His eyes are red, his breath smells, his beard is a few days old, his hair is sticking out in all directions, and he doesn't care. He looks you over, stares you down, and with the nastiest voice you can imagine spits out, "What the [bleep] do you want?!"

As you try to recover your strength, you hear a noise in the background and look past him. You see a woman in the back room throwing her clothes into a suitcase, a look of anger on her face, but also tears. You hear obscenities flying this way relentlessly and real-ize they come from a teenage boy who has no respect for the man in front of you. You are reminded of why you are here, and you muster the strength to say, "I was just in this neighborhood, and I felt that I should come to your door and ask if I can pray for you. That's all. I have nothing to sell. I just felt that this home needed prayer."

You suddenly see a completely different man. Before, he was cov-ering his weakened condition with aggression, but his hardened ex-terior is cracked, and he now appears vulnerable. He says, "Yeah, you can [bleepin'] pray for me." In a few minutes, you discover that this man is about to lose his family, his home, and his job, all because al-cohol has consumed him. He accepts Jesus as a last desperate chance. His changed life is noticeable to all almost instantly. The rest of the family is also hoping for one last chance. Within a short time, his wife and son come to Christ as well. What do you do next?

You do *not* take him out of his community and add him to your church. You assume that a church is about to start here in this neighborhood. All the neighbors immediately notice a difference in this man as he goes from door to door to apologize. They see the family change, and the Gospel message takes on a new level of power in their eyes. A few neighbors come to Christ.

There are many other guys, just like him, who used to come to the party every day. Some of their lives are also circling the drain, and they are drawn to a last chance as well. Soon, not only has a church started in the house that used to have a different sort of party, but other churches start in other homes that were equally devastated by sin and havoc.

I have tested Jesus' plan, and I must say, over and over it has come out this way. Here is one example.

Michael is a painter in Long Beach, California. He owns a business, called Michael's Painting. He was also once a drug addict. His house was a constant party. People knew that if they ever wanted to party, Michael's house was the place to find drugs and good times. Everything seemed good for Michael, until his speed habit took over. Soon everything began to fall apart. His truck (which is important for a painter) was repossessed, his business fell into bankruptcy, his home went into foreclosure, and his wife left him. Michael fell on his knees in his living room and said, "Lord, I give up!" and gave his life to Christ. God has graciously restored everything Michael lost—and more, much more.

Now, Michael's house is a church, a people of purpose. This church started six years ago, and the members have given birth to twenty other churches. They have sent out church planters who have moved to Portland, San Francisco, Salt Lake City, Indiana, France, Jordan, Kosovo, and North Africa. The church in Michael's house has only fifteen to twenty people coming regularly, yet it has "missions" that are more extensive than those of most megachurches.

This is also my church, so let me tell you about some of the people at Michael's as I look around the room. This church is different from most churches. It is always reaching new people and sending new people. Next year many of the stories and faces will have changed, but the passionate calling will not. Here are a few of the people that are a part of my church.

Michael, who hosts the church with his wife, Carlita, started a church meeting on Monday nights by reaching out to his employees.

From there, a second church began on Friday nights made up mostly of Chileans. Both churches are conducted in Spanish.

Carlita has started a weekly evangelistic outreach into a housing project in urban North Long Beach. This is one of the most dangerous pieces of real estate in Southern California. Violent crimes occur there regularly. But Carlita and Kevin have a strong sense of compassion for the children there. The person of peace that sponsored them into the community has been shot in the past—twice. In the head.

Kevin plays the guitar for us and is starting evangelistic Bible clubs on campus at Long Beach City College. He was once in a legalistic group, almost cultlike, and now he enjoys his freedom in Christ. He has much compassion for people in the bondage of cults and has led several to the same freedom that he enjoys. He is also, as I mentioned, involved in an outreach to the housing projects with Carlita in North Long Beach every week.

Elise became a Christian a short time ago and has already started a church in her new apartment. She has a heart to see souls saved and is always praying for new friends and family to come to Christ. Two of her brothers have already come to church a few times, and we are all praying for them.

Jake used to claim that he had been in jail in every county in Southern California. One day, he lost his job and decided to head to the beach. On his way, he stopped to get a six pack and some pot to cover the pain he felt. He was bodysurfing at a dangerous spot in Newport Beach when he hit his head on the bottom and came up face-down, paralyzed, drowning in a few inches of water. He says he then heard the Lord whisper in his ear, "Jake, you cannot save yourself." He surrendered to the Lord and was ready to die. A junior lifeguard trained in emergency treatment came, turned him over, immobilized him, and had someone call for the paramedics. They flew him to a hospital, where he was miraculously healed by God. He walked out of the hospital with a slight limp to remind him of his need to continue trusting in Jesus. He has been with me starting a church in East Los Angeles.

Sean now plays saxophone in our church and is writing new praise songs. He started a church meeting in a coffeehouse just around the corner from the very coffeehouse where we first met. It is made up of kids with backgrounds similar to his own. He also began a church that met at three in the morning in Downtown L.A., where he served as a security guard. Whereas once he was a thief, now he is protecting other people's property and starting churches.

Alexander, who is bound to a wheelchair because of a stroke, is reaching out at the care facility where he lives. We had to make room for two wheelchairs when his friend Valerie began coming each week to praise the Lord. Alexander, in a wheelchair, baptized Valerie, also in a wheelchair and blind. It was quite a sight. Valerie has recently gone to be with the Lord, and we miss her. We look forward to seeing her again—and to be seen by her.

Ahmed came to Christ as a Palestinian and then led his cousin Mark to the Lord. Now Ahmed has been sent to Kosovo to work and make other disciples. I will tell you more of his story in the last chapter.

Allison, who was used to help lead Ahmed to Christ, feels a strong call to minister to Muslims. Now she is working in Amman, Jordan.

Monique went to Cuba with a team of young people to train pastors to do Life Transformation Groups and theological education. The method is simple and reproducible, and she trained seven hundred pastors while convincing the Cuban government to sanction it. She has gone on several international mission trips.

Grant came to Christ a year ago. He repented of a life of homosexuality. He now has AIDS and is living a celibate life pursuing Christ. I meet weekly with Grant and am amazed at how he is so full of the Lord. He should be an angry man, but he is not. Twenty-one years earlier, he moved from the rural Midwest to New York City. He was drugged and gang-raped at a party and contracted the HIV virus that eventually became AIDS. The good news is that God has kept him alive for more than twenty-one years. When I met him, he was taking some forty medications every day. In our time together, I have watched him wean himself off many of the meds. He often feels quite strong, and now he is constantly telling others about Christ. But Grant is caught in a place where he feels hated from both sides. On one side he faces conservative Christendom who cannot understand him and are unable to accept him because of his internal desires. On the other side he faces his old homosexual friends who also won't accept who he is in Christ and ridicule him for renouncing the life he used to lead. He has many reasons to be bitter and angry. He is hated by both sides of the issue, sick with a lethal disease that was forced upon him against his will, and he must remain celibate for the days that remain to him. He is not, however, angry. He is full of the Lord and is a man of grace and forgiveness. God is transforming him into the image of Christ daily, and I learn from him weekly.

There are more stories than these. There are others who have gone on to start new works. When church is made up of lives that have experienced the transformation of the Gospel, it is full of life and more easily reproductive. This is probably the most beautiful expression of God's Kingdom I have personally ever been a part of.

At any one time we have counted up to seven mother tongues represented in this small church. We have a couple of people in their sixties and seventies, and we have a couple of toddlers wandering from lap to lap during our worship and prayer time. We have four or five youths as well as four or five families. This church is diverse, on fire, and constantly changing. People are saved, and people are sent.

The word on the street is the same; if you want to join the party, go to Michael's house. The difference now is that you get the ultimate high; you have an active part of God's Kingdom expansion. There is nothing greater.

Part Five

THE CALL TO
ORGANIC CHURCH

One scene in the last film of the *Lord of the Rings* trilogy that always excites me is when Elrond, the Elf King, visits Aragorn. Aragorn is the heir to the throne of men but has lived his life in the shadows as a lonely ranger who walks the earth. On the eve of battle, Aragorn has a nightmare and awakens to find that Elrond has visited him. At one point, Elrond pulls out the reforged sword of his ancestor, which was used to defeat the enemy hundreds of years before. He looks Aragorn directly in the eye and says in a commanding voice, "It is time to put aside the Ranger and become what you were born to be!"

A new sense of authority comes over Aragorn, a kingly aura that was only seen in small glimpses before. He takes the sword and rules men and spirit-beings alike, leading them to a victory against overwhelming odds.

This final part is a call to put aside the old life and join the epidemic of God's Kingdom. You were meant to be part of something so much more. You are royalty. Put aside the old identity and become the royalty you were born again to be.

13

FALLING WITH STYLE

Success is how high you bounce when you hit bottom.

—*Gen. George Patton*

Failure is only the opportunity to more intelligently begin again.

—*Henry Ford*

Buzz Lightyear stands on the pinnacle of a bedpost that looms over the floor like a tall skyscraper. With a fist held defiantly in the air, he boldly announces, "To infinity and beyond!" In absolute faith he leaps from the height. He believes he is a real space ranger on a mission to a strange new world. He believes he can fly. After Buzz zips around the room on Hot Wheel tracks, roller skates, a bouncing beach ball, and a ceiling fan, he lands confidently and acrobatically on the bed he left behind and proudly announces that he can fly. Woody, a toy cowboy, says to Buzz (in Tom Hanks's distinctively whiny voice), "That's not flying, it's . . . falling with style!"

Falling with style is a good philosophy of life. Our best lessons have come as we hit the ground in an attempt to fly. Everybody falls. Some do so with style, and some do not. If you're going to fall, you might as well do it with style. This chapter is written to help you feel comfortable in your attempts to lift off and yet fall with style.

It is amazing but true that offering a whole chapter about failures actually can induce hope. More than simply "misery loves company," it is helpful to know that the people involved in success stories are real people with their own weaknesses. I want you to know that not only have we made mistakes but in fact we have learned more by failure than by success. I want you to be able to learn from our mistakes as well, and feel brave enough to learn from your own failures.

One interesting piece of information is that in 1992 I was assessed by Dr. Charles Ridley (the premier church planter assessment expert[1]) to see if I could be a church planter. I failed the assessment. He wrote a kind report, but there was no doubt that, according to the best expert available, I would fail in starting a church.

Since that time, I have started many churches and trained hundreds of church planters, not because the assessment was wrong but in fact because it was right. I had to grow and overcome areas of weakness in order to become a real church planter, and Ridley saw that. I learned through this that if we accept our first assessments as failures and give up, we will miss so much. Fortunately for us all, we get more than one assessment in life.

Surrendering Our Plans to the Lord of the Harvest

When I was first called to facilitate church planting, I was director of a task force selected to start a church planting committee for our regional denominational group of churches in Southern California and Arizona in 1990. We developed a mission statement and some clear objectives. We then went away on a retreat to seek the Lord for a vision for what we should attempt in the next ten years. At the retreat we developed a ten-year plan that took into consideration what we call the multiplication factor. Our goal at the time seemed way beyond the possible unless our churches multiplied. We wanted to plant fifty churches by the year 2001.

When we returned from the retreat with what we thought was a big vision and little money, we were shocked to find that a gift was designated for us that amounted to a million dollars. This was quite a confirmation of our new vision. So we launched out, searching for church planters.

We wanted an early success that would encourage more partic-ipation from the local churches in our area, so we invested a lot of money in a single church plant. We recruited two capable church planters to work as a team, and we agreed to support them full-time in the first year. They were both evaluated personally by Ridley, and unlike me both passed the assessment. We also sent a couple of in-terns along to be trained so that they could launch the first daugh-ter churches from this plant within a couple of years. The church planting couples both went to the Church Planter's Bootcamp, put on by the Church Multiplication Training Center,[2] and both had experienced coaches. The planters and their coaches were all part of our monthly New Church Incubator[3] and religiously followed the materials found in the Church Planter's Toolkit.[4]

This team selected a growing community with much new hous-ing, conducted a demographic survey, and designed an appropriate outreach strategy. Close to thirty people who were valued leaders in two churches relocated to be part of this work. They had a good worship team and prepared children's workers and programs.

We sent out thousands of full-color, glossy brochures to homes in the area inviting families to a baseball clinic with Major League Baseball stars. Later we also did a clinic with some professional soc-cer stars as well. Many came to these events, and a good number of people attended the inaugural service. We had great anticipation for this expensive church plant. We spent more than $100,000 and mobilized thirty-plus high-caliber leaders in this church plant in a single year.

I am describing all this to you to let you know that we did everything right, according to conventional wisdom. A year later the church plant was closed. The church planters were scrambling to find secular employment, and many of the families were finding their way back to their mother churches. For all intents and pur-poses, this was a very expensive failure. But in fact it was a valuable lesson that was well worth the expense. We learned that planting churches is not about how much money or people you spend on the project. Even if everything is done right, the church may not succeed.

This experience led us to investigate what the Bible says about starting and expanding the Kingdom of God. It was about this time that I began developing Life Transformation Groups and studying the New Testament parables for how the Kingdom of God begins and expands.

Our next church plant incorporated much of our learning. It was a more organic approach, in Phoenix, where we started a cell-based church plant under the coaching of Ralph Neighbor. We were planting this church with the seeds of relational evangelism and the formation of small groups for church life. In this case, the church planter scored one of the highest assessments Ridley has given. Our vision for this church was also great, and we hoped to have a church with tens of thousands in attendance.

This did become quite a fruitful church plant, but the vision for thirty thousand people attending was not close to what God had in mind. The cell church evolved and became a network of small organic churches that spread across Phoenix and has since parented other organic church networks as well. Once again, our vision was not what God had in mind, but we are glad for that.

After this we went into a two-year drought. Not a single church planter came forward. This was a rather awkward place to be because I was about to publish a new resource on *Raising Leaders for the Harvest*[5] with my coauthor Bob Logan. My embarrassment hit its peak (or maybe trough) when Bob and I were asked to come and speak about developing church planters to all the church planting leaders for my own denomination. I remember waking early the morning I was to give my presentation, feeling foolish. How could I be an expert on developing leaders when for two straight years we had not started a single church because of a lack of leaders? I am not one to hide such an obvious dichotomy and pretend that things are fine. I went out for a cup of coffee, and while I was reading in Proverbs I asked God why we were not seeing any leaders arise and why we were so far off in our vision. There seemed to be no way now for our vision of fifty churches by 2001 to become a reality.

I read Proverbs 16:3, which said, "Commit your plans to the Lord and He will establish your works." My Bible indicated that the

Hebrew word for *commit* literally means "roll." My problem seemed to be that I would often hand my plans to the Lord but keep my hand on them at the same time. This verse hit me like a freight train. When you roll something, you have to let go of it. You can't keep a hand on it and take it back. With abject humility, somewhere in the middle of Pennsylvania, I rolled all our plans, vision, and strategy to the Lord. He gladly took them, and then He took me on the ride of my life.

I had a sense, almost immediately, that if no one else was going to plant a new church, I would. This also would address another source of pain in my credibility. I was teaching about church planting but had never actually done it. A poor assessment earlier in my life had closed the door on that.

So one of the first things I did was schedule another assessment with Charles Ridley. I could have found another person, but if the reports had come out differently I would always have wondered which one was right. Instead, I wanted the same eyes and mind looking me over. If this was from God, He would give me the green light.

My second assessment came back very positive. The shortcomings for which I was declined before had been corrected and actually become strengths.

I mentored a leader in my church, which helped me close the credibility gap I faced earlier regarding developing leaders. Then I moved my family to Long Beach and started our church.

At the advice of some experts, I recruited a strong team. I had a few people turn me down; a few said yes initially but later said no; and a few said yes and followed through. The most surprising participants were not the people that I hand-selected and recruited. There were a few folks who just joined us on their own. I did not initially see their strengths. Within a couple of years, those I personally recruited were all doing other things; those whom I did not recruit stuck it out and turned out to be the strongest team members, and several are still at it.

Karen, a woman I did not even know in the beginning, packed up her things and moved across the country to join us. She ended up being one of our strongest leaders. She learned to play guitar and became a worship leader. For the first five years of our church planting, she was the real shepherd of our Awakening Chapels.

Our original vision for the church would get an A+ from any strategic planning coach. We did our homework and had a great plan. The only one who did not like our plan was the Lord of the harvest. Needless to say, we never did fulfill our original vision.

It is possible to see early success and stop learning. The common wisdom is, "Why tamper with success? If it ain't broke, don't fix it." This can be a fatal mistake that keeps you from seasons of your greatest fruitfulness.

Our first church plant in Long Beach, though not what we had envisioned, was more than we dreamed of. We saw many conversions come quickly, and each new Christian was bringing others to Christ. The atmosphere was electric. People came from all over the world to see what God was doing.

In spite of this success, I knew we had more to learn, so I was not satisfied. We made a few adjustments with each new church plant, and we found more and more fruitfulness as we did.

When I launched out as a church planter, the first time was with a team of twelve leaders. We met in my home. This first church had a couple of daughter churches. Despite its early fruitfulness and fertility, this church continued meeting only five years. Our second church plant was a smaller team made up mostly of new converts with a couple of mature leaders. It met in one leader's apartment, had a couple of daughter churches, and continued meeting for a year. When these churches stopped meeting, most of the members were assimilated into other churches we started.

Our third church started with just a couple of brand-new believers and me. We met in Michael's home; he was fresh out of drug trafficking. We did not have a worship leader, nor did we have any other mature Christians in the beginning. This has become our most fruitful church by far, with twenty daughter churches in five years.

I am so grateful that we did not stop with the first church's success. I have come to realize that lessons learned the hard way are better than successes. I will recount many of these lessons in this chapter.

The amazing thing is that God honored our original goals, and more than fifty churches were planted by 2001. After we gave up on our vision, and I rolled the plans over to Jesus, He began to show us how to do church planting.

For several years, we had a vision of starting churches in Las Vegas. We cast that vision, made plans, and recruited many leaders. We made regular trips to the desert town, like spies checking out the Promised Land.

Not a single leader would go there. Instead, one church-planting couple went to San Francisco and another to Portland. *Our* plan was the desert wilderness, but God wanted to take the port cities along the Pacific Coast first. His plan was something more than ours. He wanted us to take the cities that were the starting place for everything that floods into the nation and everything that is exported out into the Pacific Rim.

As our movement started to gain momentum, we found that another team of young people had already started a network of organic churches in Las Vegas, and soon they were joining our movement.

It is not a bad thing to have goals and develop a strategy. It is a terrible thing if those plans take precedence over hearing God's voice and following His lead. I have never been disappointed in God's plans, but I have often been disappointed in my own. In this particular case, the Lord of the harvest showed us that He can build His Church in ways that we are not aware of.

Sharing the Sins of Others

A few of the early mistakes we made could have been avoided with simple common sense. We were so enthusiastic and eager that often we tried to push things too fast.

In our haste to have more churches, I commissioned a leader (who had been a believer for quite some time) to start a church. Unfortunately, he was lacking spiritual substance in his life because he was more interested in his own desires than those of the Lord's.

I distinctly remember laying hands on him and commissioning this work and hearing the Holy Spirit whisper in my heart, "Do not lay hands upon anyone too hastily and thereby share responsibility for the sins of others" (1 Tim. 5:22). The verse was not in my mind until that very moment, and in my deepest heart I knew it was the Lord speaking to me. Nevertheless I brushed it aside as my own imagination, ignored it, and went on with the plan.

Within a few weeks, the leader had sinned and also caused another in the church to sin. He was removed from leadership. He responded well to the discipline and has stayed with our churches, though not in leadership. He has never shown the spiritual substance needed to lead, and if I had waited longer I would have seen that.

But I also had to repent to the church publicly alongside him because, in a very real sense, I shared responsibility for his sin. The discipline was for me as much as for him. I am grateful for forgiveness and restoration just as much as he is. It is possible, in the heat of a movement, to get caught up in the apostolic sense of building Christ's Church and feel as if you cannot make a mistake.

It is common in a fast-growing, pioneering work to give too much responsibility to weak leaders, but it is also possible to start churches with leadership that is too strong. What I mean is that many leaders do not share the ministry well with others. Several of our early churches started strong and ended fast, because they were leader-dependent and those leaders were not empowering others in the church.

In these churches, the leader conducted all the evangelism, baptisms, and teaching. He became a one-man show. The rest of the church members became passive recipients with an unhealthy dependency. Once the leader moved on, the church ended.

I recognized the problem and counseled the leader to avoid it, but I was less than convincing. Perhaps that is as much a commentary on my leadership as on theirs. Churches that were leader-dependent for all of ministry did not have the health to continue and soon fizzled out. Our second and fourth churches were like this.

Some new converts initiated a church to reach out to the homeless in a park in downtown Long Beach. One of our stronger leaders took the lead; it was more of a traditional church. It actually met on Sunday mornings, which was a first for us. The team would feed the people sack lunches, play worship songs, and then preach a sermon. A few of the people said prayers to receive Christ, but lives were not changed and converts were not empowered to make other disciples. I knew that this work would not result in transformed lives or an indigenous church. I tried to coach the leaders to make some adjustments, but it never did take root.

I was proud of their care and some hungry bellies were filled, so I did not try to change it too much. After the leaders who were carrying the whole load of the church grew weary, it ended.

One church plant that was full of creative young people moved into an arts community and started more than a church. They started four or five businesses and maintained an art gallery. This was a cool church plant and many people around the globe took interest, but it was also an event-driven church and it wore out the workers who had to keep it going. It lasted for a few years and birthed some daughter churches that were more organic and less intensive, so it was a successful lesson on many counts.

A common mistake made by church planters is to recruit as many leaders as possible early on. Leaders are often brought into churches who do not share the same values. This proves painful a year or so down the road, when there is conflict over the direction in which the church should proceed.

Some of our early mistakes were more comical than damaging. One of our church planters had previously been a successful worship leader of a large megachurch. When he started his first church meeting in his living room, he set up a keyboard and sound system, complete with microphones and speakers. All ten people heard the songs really well, but it was a little too loud to sing along. Today he has a healthy network of churches with more natural and participatory worship, and he looks back with laughter at his first organic church worship experience.

Perhaps the most difficult thing for most people is not the initiatives that have failed but the people who have turned back to the world. This is an unfortunate reality for all who serve the Lord.

There are even some people whose stories are dramatic and real, but unfortunately they start better than they finish.

We are always relearning the parable of the sower. So many people are just not good soil. We can expect people to fall away and not bear fruit, but that doesn't make it any less painful. Paul had Demas and Jesus had Judas. We will all have people who disappoint us in the work to which we are called. But perhaps it is the miracle that some do *not* fall away that we should keep in mind. The fact that any are transformed forever and bear great fruitfulness makes the Great Pursuit worth it.

Imagine if Barry Bonds walked up to the plate, swung on the first pitch, and missed. Imagine him cracking the bat over his thigh, cussing, and turning around to leave for the locker room as a dejected failure. That would be foolish. Every player gets to miss the ball three times before he is out. He also gets more than one chance at bat. Even the most successful baseball players fail about 70 percent of the time at bat.

This is true in serving God. You do not have to hit the ball out of the park on your first swing to be a success. Babe Ruth once said, "Never let your fear of striking out keep you from swinging the bat." Remember that we are all allowed more than one assessment in life.

If you want to do anything of significance in God's Kingdom, follow these suggestions: listen to the Lord's voice and follow that lead. Create an environment that allows failure and restores people easily. Do not invest in potential, but in provenness. You can learn from our mistakes, but I think it also wise to learn from your own. So do not be afraid to take chances and make mistakes.

Recently I was asked to describe what I would do differently if I were to start again, knowing what I know now. Here was my response.

First, I would *begin in the harvest and start small.* Don't start with a team of already-saved Christians. We think that having a bigger and better team will accelerate the work, but it doesn't. In fact, it has the opposite effect. It is better to have a team of two, since the right two makes the work even better: an apostle and prophet together will lay the foundation of a movement. The churches birthed out of transformed lives are healthier, reproductive, and growing faster. It is about this: a life changed, not about the model. Never forget that.

Second, I would *allow God to build around others*. Don't start in your own home; find a person of peace and start in that home. Read Matthew 10 and Luke 10, and do it.

Third, I would *empower others from the start*. Don't lead too much. Let the new believers do the work of the ministry without your imposed control. Let the excitement of a new life carry the movement rather than your intelligence and persuasiveness.

Fourth, I would *let Scripture, not my assumptions, lead*. Question all your ministry assumptions in light of Scripture, with courage and faith. There is nothing sacred but God's Word and Spirit in us; let them lead rather than your own experience, teachings, and tradition.

Fifth, I would *rethink leadership*. The Christian life is a process. There is not a ceiling of maturity that people need to break through to lead. Set them loose immediately, and walk with them through the process for a while. Leadership recruitment is a dead end. We are all recruiting from the same pond, and it is getting shallower and shallower. Leadership farming is what is needed. Any leadership development system that doesn't start with the lost is starting in the wrong place. Start at the beginning, and begin with the end in mind. Mentor life on life and walk with them through their growth in being, doing, and knowing. The end is not accumulated knowledge but a life of obedience that will be willing to die for Jesus. The process isn't over until there is a flat line on the screen next to the bed.

Sixth, I would *create immediate obedience in baptism*. Baptize quickly and publicly and let the one doing the evangelizing do the baptizing. The Bible doesn't command us to be baptized, but to be baptizers. It is absolutely foolish the way we hold the Great Commission over our people and then exclude them from obeying it at the same time. We need to let the new convert imprint on the Lord for protection, provision, training, and leading, rather than on other humans.

Seventh and last, I would *settle my ownership issues.* Stop being concerned about whether "your" church plant will succeed or not. It isn't yours in the first place. Your reputation is not the one on the line; Jesus' is. He will do a good job if we let him. If we have our own identity and reputation at stake in the work, we will tend to take command. Big mistake. Let Jesus get the glory and put his reputation on the line; He can take care of Himself without your help.

It is time for faith that fears inaction, not failure. It is time to stand up high, boldly announce, "To infinity and beyond!" . . . and then take the leap. You will either fly or fall with style—*and both are worth it.*

14

TALES THAT REALLY MATTERED

A ship in a harbor is safe, but that is not what ships are made for.

— *Anonymous*

Twenty years from now you will be more disappointed by the things that you didn't do than by the ones you did do. So throw off the bowlines. Sail away from the safe harbor. Catch the trade winds in your sails. Explore. Dream. Discover.

— *Mark Twain*

A ship sits elegantly in one of the busiest harbors in the world. She has been there for almost four decades, unmoved. The *Queen Mary* is a hotel, encased in a rock jetty. Tourists who come to Long Beach must see this famous attraction. But they are seeing only a faint shadow of the world-renowned ship that she once was, taking voyages all over the world. During World War II she became a true heroine and was used to transport injured military personnel. The *Queen* was meant to be out on the high seas, but now she is on the American Automobile Association's list of four-star hotels. I can see the *Queen's* tall red smokestacks from my office on the hill; she reminds me of a hollowed-out leader who dreams of days of glory long past.

We are all familiar with the tragedy of the *Titanic*, but I believe that the *Queen Mary* is another sort of tragedy. I must confess that if I had to be a ship and choose a destiny, I would rather go out in glory on my maiden voyage like the *Titanic* than be stuck rusting in a harbor, never to make another ripple in the ocean. Award-winning movies are made of one story and not the other.

Many of us are like the *Queen Mary*: safe, secure, and not what we were meant to be. As I drive to work most mornings and see the stacks of the *Queen,* it helps remind me not to settle for less than the life Christ called me to. Many of us settle for lesser lives, for stories not worth telling. We are being called to a higher story, a bigger tale that will be told in future generations. This is not a safe tale, but none of the tales worth telling are safe ones. Leave the harbor; set sail into the open waters on a journey you will neither forget nor regret!

In this last chapter, I want to tell you about the real heroes of this new movement. They are not famous and probably never will be, this side of heaven. But of course, they never set out to be famous—just significant.

These are real stories of real people who are ordinary followers of Christ, living the reality of a Kingdom life.

A Unique Response to September 11

In the days that followed September 11, 2001, Awakening Chapel was wrestling with how to respond to the threat of Muslim extremism and cells of terrorists. We figured if there was any group equipped to understand their strategy, it was an organic church multiplying movement. We understood that the attack was a spiritual strike. The terrorists were uttering prayers to their god as they flew the jet-liners into the World Trade Center and the Pentagon. We figured that this called for a spiritual response. So we went to our knees in prayer that God would bring the truth of Christ's salvation to the Muslims in our city.

A couple of women in our church wanted to do more. They went looking for a pocket of people where they could meet Muslims. They found an Arabic restaurant in Southern California where many men would hang out and talk about things. They started going there, but it was suspicious to have two single women showing up to talk to these people. So one of them got a job there as a waitress.

They met a man named Ahmed, who was a Palestinian Muslim. He was intrigued by the women's faith and the discussions they would have. One evening he decided to come to their church and see for himself what this Christianity was like. Growing up, he had been told that Christians don't take their faith seriously. They don't pray much, they don't practice their religion, and they do not take the prophet Jesus seriously. What he found was quite different from this description. These people prayed. They worshipped. They loved each other and held one another accountable to live the Christian life fully.

Within a few weeks, he accepted Christ as His Lord—out loud, in front of everyone at the church. His was a radical conversion. He began to devour large portions of the Bible. He was baptized and led his cousin to Christ.

His cousin Mark was baptized and is now in a Life Transformation Group with me. Mark tells us how he secretly sought God his whole life, and finally God found him. God will use us if we make ourselves available to Him.

Today Ahmed is in Kosovo reaching out to Muslims. The girl who brought him to Christ, Allison, has pursued her call to reach out to Muslims and has moved to Amman, Jordan; she is involved in a mission there.

Imagine what would happen if God's entire Kingdom had responded to the events of September 11 in the same way. I believe we can do much more to counter terrorism with the spiritual weapons that are not of this world than with the arsenal deployed in Afghanistan and Iraq.

A Produce Grocer Bears Real Fruit

Harry worked in the produce department at a local grocery store. He had been a Christian for a while but was usually in the background at church events, unnoticed. Harry's is not an up-front personality. He is quiet, even withdrawn.

When Darrell started a new organic church, it was a chance for Harry to be part of a more intimate community. He started meeting with Darrell in an LTG. Then he noticed something new. The people at work started asking him to pray for them. There were other Christians at the job, people more outspoken than Harry. But Harry had a noticeable spiritual strength that was emerging. He asked Darrell what he should do with this. Darrell said, "Pray for them." He did. He started an organic church with coworkers and family members meeting in his home.

Then in a work accident Harry's foot was badly broken, and he was put out of work for some time. On disability he spent more time praying, reading his Bible, and reaching out to his family, which was spread out over fifty miles of inland Southern California. Harry is one of fifteen brothers and sisters, and he himself has several grown kids. One of his kids opened their home and a church was started. Then his mother asked if he could do the same in her home.

Within a year and a half, Harry had stared about six churches, from Riverside to Azusa (about fifty miles), meeting in homes of family members or their friends. Souls were turning to Christ, whether for the first time or back for a renewed relationship. Harry would hobble from house to house leading people to Christ and starting organic churches.

But something was wrong with Harry's foot. It was not healing properly. Then other symptoms began to show themselves. After some diagnosis, it was discovered that he had Lou Gehrig's disease.

Harry and all who love him were naturally disappointed, but he still glowed with life. He has not slowed down, though now he must be driven to the churches he has started. He has been forced to train others to lead. He is often surrounded by people in his small apartment, where he speaks with them from his wheelchair. Harry is always full of infectious joy despite physical weakness.

One of his kids had a friend who was involved with drugs and gangs. In trying to take his own life, this young man was left in a deep coma. Harry and two of his grown kids went to the hospital to visit him. When they arrived they were told that the doctors determined the young man to be brain dead and would never awaken. They were now keeping his body alive for the organs that could save other lives.

Harry placed his weak hand on the man and prayed that God would somehow be glorified by all of this. Then they went down to the cafeteria for a meal. Before they left the hospital, they went up once again to say goodbye to their friend. When they entered his room, he was sitting up in bed, alert and eating a Popsicle! This was the beginning of a new church in an area known as Moreno Valley.

Harry has become a beloved church planter and is no longer serving in the produce department. He now cares for a sort of fruit that lasts eternally. He personifies the new leader for our movement, an ordinary man with obvious weaknesses who is used by the Lord for extraordinary works.

Now My Family Is Getting into the Act

While doing some teaching in Japan, I had a dream that Heather, my daughter, started a church. In the dream, a room was full of young people who were all seriously worshiping God. When I returned from the trip, I mentioned it to her just to let her know that she was on my mind and in my dreams while I was away.

The next day she said, "Dad, my friends all want to do it!" "Do what?" I asked. "Start a church." I told her that she would have to do most of the work, and I would coach and lead only a little. She said that was fine. The next day she arranged a house to meet in, picked a night of the week, and found a worship leader; flyers were soon being passed out to friends on campus.

After the church had been meeting for several months, I met with these students and we all sang praises to the Lord. I felt the Lord's pleasure. I asked the students what was the biggest church they had ever been to. Living in Southern California there are many options of megachurches, and a number of churches were mentioned, ranging in size from two thousand attendees to more than fifteen thousand.

I then told them that I think Satan is more intimidated by this little church of fifteen high school kids than by any of those Godzilla-sized churches. They all sort of chuckled and looked around the room at one another with smiles.

I showed them why I thought this way: "How many of you think you could start a church like one of those megachurches?" No one raised a hand. I asked, "How many of you think you could start a church like this one?" and all raised their hands. I asked them to look around the room at all the raised hands, and I said with a new-found soberness, "I assure you, Satan is terrified by this."

Hey, if a fifteen-year-old girl can do this, how about you?

That Sort of Thing Never Happens to Me!

I once spoke at a missions conference in London that was designed to inspire young people from a variety of European nations to plant churches in some of the leading cities of Europe. There were students from France, England, Portugal, Germany, and the United States. I was asked to teach on the power of prayer. I didn't want to use guilt or shame in getting the people to pray more, but rather to woo them to it. So I shared many dramatic examples of the powerful ways God answered the prayers of ordinary Christians.

After I finished, a young Portuguese girl named Rachel came up to me in some distress because her own life experience did not have such dramatic accounts. In tears, she said, "My life does not have any stories in it like the ones you shared." At first I felt bad, as though I had done the very thing I did not want to do. I wanted to help her but did not really have anything valuable to say, except of course to pray. We prayed, and then I arranged to meet with her the next morning for breakfast, hoping I would come up with better ideas after some rest.

That night, many of the young students from the several countries decided to hit the streets with prayer, guitars, and Bibles. Rachel was with them. One of the young men stood on the street playing his guitar and singing. Others pretended to stop and listen. As a crowd began to form one of the students preached Christ. I later suggested that the next time they lay the guitar case open and make some money while they were at it, but they weren't interested in that. (What's wrong with the values of young people today?)

After playing on the streets, they went into a seedy club in Soho. A seductive woman came out dancing and singing a jazzy song and flirting with the men in the bar. One might wonder why our young people would go to such a place. People also wondered why Jesus used to go to such places (Matt. 9:9–13). I think you would be amazed to see what God can do when we do decide to go to the places where the sinners hang out.

After sitting in silent prayer for a time, one of the students was not feeling well, so the group started to leave. The woman who had been singing noticed the guitar and asked the young man, Claude, to sing. He gladly obliged and sang a song he had written, called "Why I Believe." Everyone applauded.

Thinking that God had done a good job, the students started to leave again. The woman, however, for virtually no reason at all, asked Rachel if she would like to sing a song. A song popped into Rachel's mind that would be perfect for this situation but she couldn't remember all the lyrics, so she declined. The woman insisted. Rachel got up and began to sing. She said that the Lord gave her new lyrics to fill in for those she couldn't remember, as well as a bold confidence within herself. When she was done, the whole place was silent and every jaw hung open in amazement. Some of the other students said later that it was the most beautiful song they had ever heard. They imagined heaven sounding this way.

The crowd wanted to hear more, but the students had to leave (it was very late). As they walked out, the seductive woman asked Rachel if she would pray for her. Rachel was more than willing to oblige; she now had a new respect for the power behind her own prayers.

All this occurred unbeknownst to me. The next morning, I sat next to Rachel at breakfast to try to help her with her prayer life. She stopped me midsentence and explained all that had occurred the night before. Wow, I thought, I guess she doesn't really need my help after all. Isn't it amazing what can happen if we just pray?

Perhaps you feel the way Rachel did when you hear such stories.

Could it be that there is a nagging thought in your own soul, like a splinter in your mind driving you mad? Is there a doubt about the normal life you have been living? Do you feel that you were meant to be a part of something much more? If you look over your own life and recognize that it does not have the powerful and life-changing tales in it like those that are contained in this book, then take the red pill. Venture out of the harbor and launch into deeper and unsafe waters. You will not be disappointed, and you certainly will not be bored.

A couple of years ago, I was teaching many of these principles in Osaka, Japan. A woman came up to me afterward in tears. She spoke no English at all, and I do not speak any Japanese (my translator was not available). That did not stop her. She started pouring out her heart to me, explaining something obviously important and weeping as she did. I did not understand her words, but the Spirit was telling me in my heart that she was feeling woefully inadequate in her spiritual life—much as Rachel did in Europe. This woman was feeling that her Christian life was unimpressive. So I volunteered to pray for her. She understood what I intended and allowed me to place my hand on her shoulder and lift her to the Lord. She did not understand what I was praying in words, but I think her spirit did, much as mine had a sense of what she was telling me. I prayed that the Lord of the harvest would help her see people around her that she could influence with the Gospel and lead to Christ. I asked God to grant her significance and use her to start a chain reaction with the Gospel where she worked. Somehow, I knew she was a nurse at a hospital.

Over a year later, I was teaching again in Osaka. This woman came up to me again, but this time she had an English-speaking friend with her and a smile rather than tears. Her friend was also a nurse but from another hospital many kilometers away in another city. I was told that this nurse I prayed for had led this other woman to find Christ out of New Age mysticism and the occult. The first woman then transferred to another hospital and had since led other nurses to Christ. A little over a year since I first met this nurse, there are now five nurses who have all come to Christ. Both women were all smiles. Jesus had answered her prayers and begun to fulfill her heart's desire. He can do so with you as well.

A sophomore girl in high school, a painter, a grocer, and a nurse. This is not the type of hero we are used to in great stories. I think that is what makes the stories even better. These are people like you. You can lead a heroic life of significance as well.

I believe we are leaving the day of the *ordained* and ushering in the day of the *ordinary*. It is a time when common Christians will do uncommon deeds because God delights in using weak and foolish things to shame the world. Do not settle for a lesser life. If you start on this journey and set sail for deeper waters, you will come under attack. You will join the ranks of those that the enemy cannot ignore, and he will fight against you with unfair tactics.

In *Lord of the Rings*, surrounded by the ruins of buildings that once were glorious and now are ghosts, the hobbit Frodo feels a call in his flesh to surrender the power he carries embodied in the ancient ring of Sauron. As if in a dream, a voice calls him to a lie, and he turns to follow the voice and give the ring of power to a dark king who rides a dragon.

We all know these weaknesses. In this scene from *Lord of the Rings: The Two Towers*, there is no better depiction in all of film of the spiritual world in which we find ourselves. In vivid reality, it shows us that we are truly simple folk drawn into a story way too big for us. We face three enemies: the world, the flesh, and the devil, and each is portrayed in graphic realism in this incredibly powerful scene. Perhaps this movie fantasy portrays the truth around us in the invisible world more realistically because the truth is more like a fantasy world than this "matrix" world we call real that has been pulled down over our eyes.

Frodo walks slowly up some stairs to the top of a parapet and begins to surrender to his own flesh as it calls out to darkness.

A dark witch king, more ghost than man, rides on a dragon in front of Frodo to take the ring and destroy the simple hobbit with one slicing grip of its serpent talons.

Just as the enemy is about to seize the victory, Sam, Frodo's faithful companion, pulls him back to freedom. They struggle for a moment, because we often forget who our friends are—and worse yet, who our enemy is. Once Frodo recognizes Sam, he drops his sword, falls back on his haunches, and tells Sam he can't continue with his quest. Sam understands; he knows that they shouldn't even be in this situation, but there they are. The real truth is that we were meant to rule in a paradise, and we should not be here in this corrupt world of degradation and temptation. But here we are. We are in the midst of a great epic battle between good and evil, like simple hobbits who should never have to play so heroic a role against such overwhelmingly powerful darkness.

How can these small rural hobbits be so important in the outcome of epic events of global significance? It is precisely their simple and ordinary lives that make them so powerful. Less inclined to be seduced by power and prestige, they are uncommonly resistant to temptation. God delights when He can use the weak and foolish things of the earth to shame the mighty and wise.

From this dark moment, a light shines. A friend lifts up his brother and inspires hope. Frodo regains perspective, and the journey continues.

Sam goes on to give an inspiring speech. Frodo is lifted from his lonely place of defeat and despair. We all need a friend who helps us remember why this journey into battle is worth the cost.

Sam says:

It's like the great stories, Mr. Frodo, the ones that really mattered. Full of darkness and danger they were. And sometimes you didn't want to know the end, because how could the end be happy? How could the world go back to the way it was when so much bad had happened? But in the end it's only a passing thing, this shadow. Even darkness must pass. A new day will come. And when the sun shines, it will shine out the clearer. Those were the stories that stayed with you, that meant something. Even if you were too small to understand why. But I think, Mr. Frodo, I do understand. I know now.

Folks in those stories had lots of chances of turning back, only they
didn't. They kept going because they were holding on to something.

"What are we holding on to, Sam?" Frodo sighs, still overcome
by the near defeat of the previous moment.

In determination to help his brother for whom he would gladly
die, Sam lifts Frodo to his feet, looks him sternly in the eye, and
says, "That there's some good in this world, Mr. Frodo, and it's
worth fighting for."

We all need a friend like Sam when we face the overwhelming
odds of this battle we are in. We also need to be a friend like Sam.
The struggle against the evil that dominates the world is bad enough;
to go through this fight alone is too much. We must have a small
band of brothers and sisters who would give their lives for us, for the
cause, for Jesus.

Yes, there is conflict. Yes, there is evil that wants only to destroy
you. Yes, there will be pain and loss. But the struggle is worth it.
Any great story has conflict; this is what makes the story worth the
telling. There would not be three major motion pictures, dozens of
Oscars, and a billion dollars in revenue if there were no struggle involved with the *Lord of the Rings* tales. If the Hobbits never left
home but stayed in the Shire, under the party tree smoking pipe
weed, we would not really be all that interested in the stories. The
conflict makes the struggle compelling.

If we can stick together and pull each other through, much like
Sam and Frodo, I believe we can defeat the enemy and win this war.
There will be great stories to tell our children's children. These are
the days when grocers, high school kids, nurses, and simple garden-
ers, like Sam, overcome incredible evil to bring change and hope
back to humanity.

This is what you were born to be: a hero. You were created for
good works that have been foreordained by God to destroy evil
strongholds and set captives free. Do not settle for rusting in the
harbor over the decades. Set sail on the oceans of risk, and let God
lead you to stories that are worthy of being told.

Notes

Introduction

1. McNeil, R. *The Present Future Church*. San Francisco: Jossey-Bass, 2003, p. 4.
2. Moberly, Sir W. *The Crisis in the University*. London: SCM Press, 1953.
3. Newbigin, L. *The Gospel in a Pluralistic Society*. Grand Rapids, Mich.: Eerdmans, 1989, p. 230.

Chapter One

1. Silvoso, E. *That None Should Perish*. Ventura, Calif.: Regal, 1997, p. 100.
2. Logan, R. E., and Clegg, T. *Releasing Your Church's Potential*. Saint Charles, Ill.: ChurchSmart Resources, 1998, pp. 4–12.

Chapter Two

1. Logan, R., and Cole, N. *Raising Leaders for the Harvest*. Saint Charles, Ill.: ChurchSmart Resources, 1995.
2. Further explanation is found in my book *Cultivating a Life for God* (Saint Charles, Ill.: ChurchSmart Resources, 1999).

Chapter Three

1. Warren, R. *The Purpose Driven Church*. Grand Rapids, Mich.: Zondervan, 1995.

2. Law, W. *A Serious Call to a Devout and Holy Life*. New York: Vintage Books, 2002 (originally published in 1728), pp. 6–7. Law was an Anglican priest concerned that followers of Christ be truly transformed, not simply have a new set of rules to try to follow.

Chapter Five

1. Sider, R. J. *The Scandal of the Evangelical Conscience: Why Are Christians Living Just Like the Rest of the World?* Grand Rapids, Mich.: Baker, 2005.
2. Barclay, W. *The New Daily Study Bible: The Gospel of John*, vol. 1. Louisville, Ky.: Westminster John Knox Press, 2001, p. 195

Chapter Six

1. Allen, R. *Spontaneous Expansion of the Church and the Causes That Hinder It*. Grand Rapids, Mich.: Eerdmans, 1962, p. 13.

Chapter Seven

1. http://www.onmission.com/webzine/mar_apr03/assisting.html.
2. "China Confronts Its Daunting Gender Gap." *Los Angeles Times*, Jan. 21, 2005, p. A6.
3. Schwarz, C. *Natural Church Development*. Saint Charles, Ill.: ChurchSmart Resources, 1996, pp. 46–48.
4. Bounds, E. M. *Power Through Prayer*. Grand Rapids, Mich.: Baker, 1972, p. 5.
5. http://www.avert.org/worldstats.htm.

Chapter Eight

1. Examine the parables found in Mark chapter 4 to see how the seed of God's word planted should result in spontaneous and expansive influence of the Kingdom of God. Note especially the parables in Mark 4:26–32.

2. Allen, R. *Missionary Methods: St. Paul's or Ours?* Grand Rapids, Mich.: Eerdmans, 1962, p. 3.

3. T. Wolf, The Universal Disciple: Prague Lectures, University Institute, San Francisco, California, 2003.

4. Wolf calls this the Universal Disciple Pattern (see the table later in the chapter).

5. Allen (1962), p. ii.

6. www.universal-disciple.com. Many of these ideas have been adapted and elaborated from Thom Wolf.

7. Gladwell, M. *The Tipping Point: How Little Things Can Make a Big Difference*. Boston: Back Bay Books, 2002, pp. 24–25.

8. Allen (1962), pp. 87–88.

9. Cole, N. *Cultivating a Life for God: Multiplying Disciples Through Life Transformation Groups*. Saint Charles, Ill.: ChurchSmart Resources, 1999.

10. 1 Cor. 11:23–26.

11. The actual warning not to take the elements of communion "in an unworthy manner" (1 Cor. 11:27–32) is for church members who are abusing the Lord's Supper for personal gain at the expense of others. It is clear that the discipline accompanying taking the supper in an unworthy manner is directed toward Christians, as Paul explains that this very punishment is one thing that separates us from the condemnation of the world (v. 32). There is no mention that this applies in any way to unbelievers who are already under a strict judgment for sin, or as Paul says, "condemnation." When we do take the communion as Jesus intended, we "proclaim His death until He comes" (1 Cor. 11:26). Even in the very first communion, when Jesus gave us the example to follow in remembrance of Him, he clearly did not exclude the unbeliever who was at the table (Luke 22:14–23; John 13:10–11).

12. Patterson, G., and Scoggins, D. *Church Multiplication Guide*. Pasadena, Calif.: William Carey Library, 1993, pp. 16–20.

13. The seven are to repent, believe, and receive the Holy Spirit; be baptized; love God and neighbor; celebrate the Lord's Supper;

pray; give; and disciple others; Patterson and Scoggins (1993), p. 17.

14. Cole, N., and Kaak, P. *The Organic Church Planters' Greenhouse Intensive Training*. Long Beach, Calif.: CMA Resources, 2003, pp. 1–6.

Chapter Nine

1. http://www.free-definition.com/Organization.html.
2. http://www.chaordic.org/learn/res_def.html.
3. Hock, D. *The Birth of the Chaordic Age*. San Francisco: Berrett-Koehler, 1999.
4. Warren (1995), p. 46.
5. A fractal is a rough or fragmented geometric shape that can be subdivided in parts, each of which is (at least approximately) a reduced-size copy of the whole (http://spanky.triumf.ca/www/fractal-info/what-is.htm).
6. I am indebted to Wayne Cordeiro for exposing me to the analogies of fractal design as well as the endoskeletal and exoskeletal systems. Cordeiro, W. *Doing Church as a Team*. Ventura, Calif.: Regal, 2001, pp. 179–180.
7. Hyde, D. *Dedication and Leadership*. Notre Dame, Ind.: University of Notre Dame Press, 1966.
8. Although it is true that Peter commanded the converts on the day of Pentecost ("Repent and let each of you be baptized"; Acts 2:38), the actual imperative that is spoken to all of us believers in Matthew 28:19–20 places the impetus for obedience to baptism not on the new convert but on the one who makes disciples.

Chapter Ten

1. MacArthur, J. *The MacArthur New Testament Commentary: Matthew 8–15*. Chicago: Moody, 1987, p. 103.
2. MacArthur (1987).

Chapter Eleven

1. http://www.cs.virginia.edu/oracle/.
2. Gladwell (2002).
3. Seligman, D. "Me and Monica: Social Network Theory Illuminates the Big Story, and a Lot More." *Forbes*, Mar. 23, 1998, pp. 76–77.
4. Gladwell (2002).
5. It was Thom Wolf who first opened up my understanding of the term and use of *oikos* and its implications for global evangelization. I am indebted to him for his keen insight and teachings. Others have passed this teaching on to the world, but it was Thom who first unlocked its riches. Of course, he would be second to Jesus.
6. Cole and Kaak (2003), pp. 2–3.

Chapter Twelve

1. Blackaby, H. *Experiencing God*. Nashville, Tenn.: Broadman and Holman, 1994.

Chapter Thirteen

1. Ridley, C. *How to Select Church Planters: A Self-Study Manual for Recruiting, Screening, Interviewing and Evaluating Qualified Church Planters*. Pasadena, Calif.: Fuller Evangelistic Association, 1988. See also Ridley, C. R., and Logan, R. E., with Gerstenberg, H. *Training for Selection Interviewing*. Saint Charles, Ill.: ChurchSmart Resources, 1999.
2. Church Multiplication Training Center (http://www.cmtcmultiply.org/bootcamp_standard.htm).
3. Logan, R. E., and Ogne, S. L. *New Church Incubator*. Fullerton, Calif.: Church Resource Ministries, 1991.
4. Logan, R. E., and Ogne, S. L. *The Church Planter's Toolkit: A Self-Study Resource Kit*. Saint Charles, Ill.: ChurchSmart Resources, 1991.
5. Logan and Cole (1995).

Acknowledgments

This book is the product of more than a decade of learning. In the process, I have been blessed to be surrounded with a great team of courageous people willing to take a chance and try something new.

To Thom Wolf, Tom Julien, George Patterson, Howard Snyder, and Robert Banks, who have blazed trails ahead of me, thank you. I stand tall on your shoulders and see what will become. Your ideas invade my mind such that your words often come out of my mouth. I pray that I will always give honor where it is due.

To Carol Davis, Wolfgang Simson, Tony and Felicity Dale, Mike Steele, John White, Robert Fitts, Jonathan Campbell, Alan Hirsch, and Curtis Sergeant: you have all contributed insight to this work and my life. I count you all as peers, coworkers, and friends.

To Bob Buford, Dave Travis, Linda Stanley, and all my friends at Leadership Network as well as those who are part of the Burning Bush group, thanks for sharpening my mind and my skills. Your support has been tremendous. God brought you to me at the right time.

To Paul Kaak: you are more than my associate. You are my brother in this work. You have walked with me, written with me, and spoken with me into this movement from the start. Paul, I value all of our late-night talks and all-day discussions. This work would be so much less without them.

To Phil Helfer, my friend and pastor, a radical thinker and loyal friend: you stimulate my mind and care for my soul. To me, you are the ideal shepherd, second only to the Great One whom we both serve.

To those who have taken these ideas and run with them coura-geously, I am deeply indebted. There are too many to mention, but there are some I must thank, or this page would not be legitimate. Ed Waken, Brad Fieldhouse, Doug Lee, Dezi Baker, Mike Jentes, Rich Hagler, Kevin Rains, Scott Wilson, Jonathan Dale, Joseph Cartwright, Harold Behr, John Macy, Greg Hubbard, Jason Evans, Shain Logeais, Robert Ferris, Luke Smith, Yoshito Ishihara, Takeshi Takazawa, Shigeru Tsukura, Mitsuo Fukuda, Kaz Endo, and the rest of the ever-increasing number of pioneers out in the fields reaping a great harvest: thank you.

To Angela Bokkes, the brain that keeps our various ministries working at CMA, I am grateful. The Lord has used you to free me up so that I may pursue things like writing and teaching about Or-ganic Church.

Val, thanks for helping with the editing. Your insights have made me seem much more smarterer than I is.

I wish to thank all those who are a part of Awakening Chapels, past and present. You may think you have learned from me, but it is actually the other way around. "I thank God in all my remem-brance of you all. . . . For it is only right for me to feel this way about you all, because I have you in my heart" (Phil. 1:3, 7).

Finally, to Dana, my wife, thanks for keeping me grounded and real.

About the Author

Neil Cole is an experienced church planter and pastor. Aside from founding the Awakening Chapels, which are reaching young postmodern people in urban settings, he is also a founder of Church Multiplication Associates (CMA), which has grown to more than seven hundred churches in thirty-two states and twenty-three nations in only six years. Currently he serves as CMA's executive director. He is responsible for resourcing church leaders with ministry tools to reproduce healthy disciples, leaders, churches, and movements. His responsibilities also include recruiting, developing, assessing, and coaching church planters.

Cole is an international speaker; has also authored *Cultivating a Life for God* and *TruthQuest;* and coauthored *Raising Leaders for the Harvest* and *Beyond Church Planting: Pathways for Emerging Churches* (publication in 2005), both with Robert Logan, and *Organic Church Planters' Greenhouse* with Paul Kaak. He lives in Long Beach, California, with his wife, Dana, and their three children, Heather, Erin, and Zachary.

Subject Index

A

Abortion clinics, 75
Accountability, and size of church, 100
Ahmed, 191, 209
Alexander, 191
Alicia, 56
Allen, R., 89, 91, 110
Allison, 191, 209
Animal House (film), 3
Antioch, local church at, 41–42
Apollo 13 (film), xix, xxvii
Apostolic mission, and DNA of church, 114–118
Aragorn, 4–5
Atlanta, Georgia, 75
Authority, delegated versus distributed, 134–137
Availability, as key to witness, 167
Awakening Chapels, 22–26, 29, 137, 152, 208–209

B

Bankruptcies, 75
Baptism, 111–112, 132–133, 205
Barney, 159–160
Basic unit, of church life, 99–103
Belushi, J., 3
Beuchner, F., 159
Bible, reading of, 65–68
The Birth of the Chaordic Age (Hock), 124
Blackaby, H., 177
Bono, 61
Borden, B., 73–74
Bounds, E. M., 96
Braveheart (film), 136
Buechner, F., xix
Buford, B., 74, 88

Buildings, and concept of Church, 35–38

C

Cadet maxim, at West Point Military Academy, 143
Canth, M., xix
Caricatures, of Church, 34–45
Carlita, 189–192
Carlos, 79–81
Carlota, 77–78, 81
Centralization, and Kingdom of God, 41–45
Chaordic, definition of, 123
Chaos theory, 123
Chicago Bulls, 54–55
China, 92
Christ. *See* Jesus
Church attendance, lack of, xx–xxi, xxii, xxiii
Church, concepts of, 5–7, 7–15, 34–45, 47–57
Church Multiplication Associates (CMA), 22, 137–140
Church multiplication movement: basic unit in, 99–103; death and, 103–105; discovery of, 17–29; DNA of church and, 113–121; parable of mustard seed and, 97–99; parable of sower and, 64–81, 84–89; reproduction of church and, 93, 96–97, 173–192; spontaneous multiplication movement and, 17, 88, 89, 113, 124–140; structure in, 126–129. *See also* Church planting
Church Multiplication Training Center, 197
Church Planter's Bootcamp, 197
Church Planter's Toolkit, 197

Scriptural Index

CMAResources seeks to identify missional principles and reproducible methods that can propagate in a variety of cultures and contexts. We aim to empower ordinary Christians to accomplish extraordinary works with the powerful gifts given by Jesus. All of our resources are focused to that end. We also want to provide a voice to the artists, authors, and pioneers of this new movement.

We believe that any resource worth producing meets the test of the following criteria. It can be

- *Received personally*. It has a profound effect in what it sets out to accomplish.
- *Repeated easily*. It is simple enough that it can easily be passed on in a short encounter.
- *Reproduced strategically*. It can be applied in a variety of cultures and contexts globally.

Our highly scrutinized list of resources helps contribute to seeing church multiplication movements internationally. Resources such as *Cultivating a Life for God*, TruthQuest: A Community-Based Doctrinal Discovery System, Life Transformation Group Cards, and *Organic Church Planters' Greenhouse* are all available exclusively at CMAResources.

Visit our Website to order resources or to find information on our training events, and don't forget to read newly posted articles dealing with organic church planting. You can also sign up to receive our weekly e-newsletter.

CMAResources
1965 E. 21st Street
Signal Hill, CA 90755
Main: (562) 961–1962
Fax: (562) 961–1982
www.cmaresources.org

Other Books of Interest

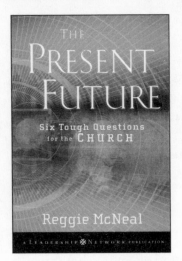

The Present Future

Six Tough Questions for the Church

Reggie McNeal

Cloth
ISBN: 0-7879-6568-5

"This is the most courageous book I have ever read on church life. McNeal nails the problem on the head. Be prepared to be turned upside down and shaken loose of all your old notions of what church is and should be in today's world."

—George Cladis, senior pastor, Westminster Presbyterian Church, Oklahoma City and author, *Leading the Team-Based Church*

"With humor and rare honesty Reggie McNeal challenges church leaders to take authentic Christianity back into the real world. He's asking the right questions to help us get back on track."

—Tommy Coomes, contemporary Christian music pioneer and record producer, artist with Franklin Graham Ministries

"Reggie McNeal throws a lifeline to church leaders who are struggling with consumer-oriented congregations wanting church for themselves. The Present Future will recharge your passion."

—Rev. Robert R. Cushman, senior pastor, Princeton Alliance Church, Plainsboro, New Jersey

In this provocative book, author, consultant, and church leadership developer Reggie McNeal identifies the six most important realities that church leaders must address including: recapturing the spirit of Christianity and replacing "church growth" with a wider vision of kingdom growth; developing disciples instead of church members; fostering the rise of a new apostolic leadership; focusing on spiritual formation rather than church programs; and shifting from prediction and planning to preparation for the challenges of an uncertain world. McNeal contends that by changing the questions church leaders ask themselves about their congregations and their plans, they can frame the core issues and approach the future with new eyes, new purpose, and new ideas.

Reggie McNeal is the director of leadership development for the South Carolina Baptist Convention. Drawing on twenty years of leadership roles in local congregations and his work over the last decade with thousands of church leaders, McNeal counsels local churches, denominational groups, seminaries and colleges, and para-church organizations in their leadership development needs. He lives in Columbia, South Carolina, with his wife and two daughters. He is the author of *A Work of Heart* from Jossey-Bass.